THE GOOD COOK
WORLD WAR II
THE TIME-LIFE ENCYCLOPAEDIA
OF GARDENING
HUMAN BEHAVIOUR
THE GREAT CITIES
THE ART OF SEWING
THE OLD WEST
THE WORLD'S WILD PLACES
THE EMERGENCE OF MAN
LIFE LIBRARY OF PHOTOGRAPHY
TIME-LIFE LIBRARY OF ART
FOODS OF THE WORLD
GREAT AGES OF MAN
LIFE SCIENCE LIBRARY
LIFE NATURE LIBRARY
YOUNG READERS LIBRARY

The World of
Bruegel

TIME-LIFE LIBRARY OF ART

The World of Bruegel

c. 1525 – 1569

by Timothy Foote
and
the Editors of TIME-LIFE BOOKS

TIME
LIFE
BOOKS

TIME-LIFE BOOKS B.V.

About the Author

Timothy Foote is a Harvard Phi Beta Kappa who studied English literature and history as an undergraduate and in the graduate school. A former writer with Time-Life Books, he has been an Associate Editor of LIFE and is now a senior editor of TIME. He first began to study the paintings of Pieter Bruegel in Europe where he lived and worked for six years, first as a foreign correspondent and finally as the editor of the International Book Society. His articles and reviews have appeared in TIME, LIFE, *The New York Times Magazine, Esquire* and the French cultural monthly *Preuves.*

The Consulting Editor

H. W. Janson is Professor of Fine Arts at New York University. Among his numerous publications are his *History of Art* and *The Sculpture of Donatello.*

The Consultant for This Book

Leonard J. Slatkes is Assistant Professor of Art History at Queens College of the City University of New York. Dr. Slatkes, who earned his doctorate at the University of Utrecht in the Netherlands, has also taught at the University of Chicago and Pittsburgh University. A specialist in Dutch and Flemish art, he is the author of a monograph on the early 17th Century master Dirck van Baburen and of studies of other artists of the period.

On the Cover

With spirited steps, a Flemish farm couple joins a lusty dance in a village street. This is a detail from Bruegel's *Peasant Dance,* which appears on pages 136-139.

End Papers

Front: Hooded and masked for safety, a small group of beekeepers tend their hives in a drawing that Bruegel made in 1568, the year before his death. *Back:* This drawing of an alchemist in his steaming studio was designed by Bruegel as the model for an engraving to be printed by his publisher, Hieronymus Cock. Through the window the alchemist's family is seen being led away to the poorhouse; the inscription, *Al ghe Mist,* on the book at the left is a pun on the word alchemist; in translation it means "all in vain."

© 1968 Time-Life Books Inc. All rights reserved.
Seventh European English language printing, 1981.

ISBN 900658 59 2

TIME-LIFE is a trademark of Time Incorporated U.S.A.

Contents

Two Views of the World: Symbol and Reality

In Pieter Bruegel's time people had heard of only one skyscraper. They would have had no trouble identifying the shambling structure at the right—the Tower of Babel. In the 16th Century, the Biblical story of man's calamitous attempt to reach heaven was a favorite symbol of pride and a familiar theme in art. Bruegel painted the subject at least three times. The fascination exerted on the public imagination by the tower, and especially by Bruegel's treatment of it, reveals much about how he and his audience saw the world.

In 16th Century Flanders the legacy of the Middle Ages was strong. The primary aim of art was still to preach Christian morality or instill pious feelings. Man was seen small, his habitual follies ruthlessly exposed. Naturally, the Bible loomed large in thought as in art. Bruegel's public could be counted on to know the popular version of the Tower of Babel story: how King Nimrod presumptuously ordered a tower that would reach the clouds, and how God punished him by making the workers speak in a babble of tongues so that the job could never be completed.

But Nimrod built in Babylon. Bruegel raised his tower outside a busy Flemish city complete with bustling seaport and step-gabled buildings. The inconsistency did not trouble his audience. Adept at seeing didactic parallels between past and present, they were perfectly prepared to find sinful pride as prevalent in 16th Century Flanders as in ancient Babylon. They were the inheritors of an artistic convention in which everything in a painting was to be judged and enjoyed both as a symbol and as an accurate portrayal of real life. And Bruegel was the ultimate master of this convention.

As the scenes on the following pages show, Bruegel's picture stirs with life. The tower is crowded with teams of workmen, stone cutters, bricklayers, even a few foraging chickens and an old crone sweeping up. Earlier painters had dramatically pictured Nimrod as an imposing monarch full of pride and deserving of his punishment. Bruegel shows him (in the left foreground) as a vain, petty dignitary whose arrival merely slows the work. Such human touches help transform a towering symbol into a portrait of everyday life, with man working at worldly enterprise —but doomed to final failure.

Tower of Babel, 1563

I

The Northern View:
Art in the Netherlands

The most famous paintings of the Italian Renaissance bear splendid witness to an ideal world. Timeless, sun-drenched, benign, it is as often peopled with gods and angels as with men. Even the earthly inhabitants tend to be majestic—great princes and philosophers strolling between Greek and Roman columns, dignified shepherds, marble-smooth ladies who go clad, if clad at all, in curls of gauze, or sit in virginal serenity with robes that always fall in perfect folds.

For centuries these shapely and spacious visions have given pleasure to the world. Indeed, the Italian masters have had such an impact on the history of art that even today they are often thought of simply as *the* painters of the Renaissance period. Yet at almost the same time they were at work in Florence and Rome creating their radiant blend of Christianity and classicism in art, a great painter was born in the north of Europe who would shape the likeness of a far different world.

The man was Pieter Bruegel. The time of his birth, about 1525, came during Michelangelo's prime, only a few years after the death of Raphael, and not long after a German monk named Martin Luther had first challenged the power of the Roman Catholic Church. The date almost coincided, as well, with the return of one of Portuguese navigator Ferdinand Magellan's ships from the first voyage around the globe.

The place of Bruegel's birth was probably a village in the duchy of Brabant just north of the border between present-day Holland and Belgium. Both of these small countries were then part of a group of 17 troubled provinces known collectively as the Netherlands. It was there, during Bruegel's lifetime, that the new Protestantism established itself. It combined with a rising sense of Dutch nationalism to defy the authority of the powerful Austrian house of Habsburg, the Catholic King of Spain and the Church of Rome. The resulting conflict, known in the Netherlands as the Eighty Years' War, was a decisive event in European history. The war finally ended with seven northern provinces of the Netherlands established as free, largely Protestant and democratic Holland. Though the rest of the provinces remained in Catholic hands, eventually becoming modern Belgium, the assembled forces of the Catholic Counter

Reformation had suffered a fateful setback. A tiny sliver of land inhabited by a handful of people had humbled the Roman Church's most powerful defenders, and the cause of Protestantism and political self-determination had been permanently enhanced.

The long war did not break out officially until 1567, two years before Pieter Bruegel's death, but it simmered toward that final explosion throughout the painter's lifetime. In the Netherlands, and especially in prosperous Flanders to which Bruegel moved as a young painter, this was an epoch when men were often forced to choose between state and religion, between old loyalties and new. Their choice frequently meant torture or loss of worldly goods, sometimes even flight to safety (and exile) in more tolerant countries like England.

It may be that the danger of having one's personal thoughts or business known to the authorities in those times accounts for the sparseness of facts now available about Pieter Bruegel. Though historians and critics have tried to assign a partisan role to the artist—he has been viewed as everything from a secret propagandist for the Protestant cause to a toady of the Catholic establishment—little is certain about Bruegel's private life. It is known that under the name Pieter Brueghel he became a master painter in Antwerp in 1551. By 1559, unaccountably, he had dropped the "h" for good, signing himself "Bruegel." After traveling to Rome to study, he established himself in Antwerp, then moved to Brussels in 1563 when he married the daughter of Pieter Coeck van Aelst, a fellow painter. Before his death in 1569 he had two sons, Pieter and Jan, who both became painters and, putting the "h" back into the family name, had children of their own to continue what became a Brueghelian painting dynasty.

Although mystery still surrounds Bruegel's reactions to the intellectual ferment and religious controversy of his age, they clearly laid their mark on his art. Not surprisingly, the world that he eventually shaped in oils, in marked contrast to the Italian view, is neither temperate nor timeless. It is, instead, weather-whipped and full of violence, by turn grotesquely cruel and comic. Unlike the Italian Renaissance painters, Bruegel saw man small. His lumpish creatures, mostly peasants and middle-class folk, are neither noble nor godlike and are often prey to strong drink and thieving habits. Muffled in clumsy clothes against the northern cold, they carouse in fear for their own brief mortality, sometimes find themselves pursued by demons and often dance, as men will do in terrifying times, within the shadow of the gallows. Like most of us, in short, they freeze in winter, sweat in summer and are foolish in all seasons.

But because the Italian ideal in art—that painting should ennoble the human figure—long held sway, Bruegel was for centuries undervalued by the men who set European art fashion as a rude "peasant" painter. It is only within fairly recent years, in fact, that Bruegel has begun to be seen for what he actually was—a complex man who was not only the greatest Flemish painter of his century but one whose extraordinary power and whose range of subject matter placed him among the handful of great painters in history. Modern viewers regard everyday life as a perfectly fitting subject for enduring art. For them it is easy to recognize in Bruegel's 40-odd paintings and over 150 drawings a pioneer attempt at showing the common man in art, as well as a fascinating and unsurpassed portrait of conditions in northern Europe in an age when life was short, strenuous and full of pain. Bruegel's pictures linger in the memory not merely because they delight the eye but because they engage the mind. Crammed with gyrating human figures and studded with every sort of homely detail, they constitute a kind of literary tapestry, which can be thoroughly read as well as briefly viewed.

The scenes of this Bruegelian tapestry have a remarkable variety of tone and subject—from good cheer to near tragedy, from grotesque Flemish fantasies and comic illustrated proverbs to landscapes so universal that they seem to be philosophic statements about the dependence of man upon nature. Most of them are sharply symbolic in illustrating the perilous situation of man as Bruegel observed it. One, *The Magpie on the Gallows,* actually shows peasants dancing under a gibbet while the fresh green leaves of spring sprout hopefully on the trees all about them. But at the simplest level many of Bruegel's pictures, like *The Battle between Carnival and Lent (pages 130-131),* offer a round-trip ticket to a 16th Century Flemish village fete. Figuratively, a viewer can walk right in and happily find himself surrounded by dozens of Mardi Gras attractions— an enormous fat Fleming riding a vast barrel and preparing to joust with a thin, blue-jowled figure got up as Lent; venders hawking waffles, prurient gawkers enjoying a knockabout comedy, aptly entitled "The Ugly Bride," being staged by strolling players.

These fairground settings and the cavorting crowds are sometimes put to more serious purpose by Bruegel. Then the indulgent irony about human foibles, which customarily infuses his pictures, sharpens toward somber judgment. One of the clearest examples is the Biblical scene shown on pages 108-111. In it Bruegelian crowds still skylark. A man sells cider. Small boys hop through the mud on stilts. But there, almost lost in the torrent of life, which swirls through the middle distance, is the tiny figure of Christ, with His Cross laid on Him, laboring toward a grove of distant gibbets. Suddenly the unsuspecting viewer, who has simply been enjoying all Bruegel's funny little people, understands the title of the picture, *The Carrying of the Cross*, and is confronted with the painter's point: Jerusalem's hill of Calvary could just as well have been a knoll outside 16th Century Antwerp.

Toward the end of his life, Bruegel's paintings became simpler and more powerful. They contained fewer and larger human figures and more space. Sometimes the result, as in the illustrated parable called *The Blind Leading the Blind,* is to sound the pessimism of an age and region that saw men in blind fury attack each other in the name of God. Sometimes Bruegel creates a massive Northern landscape and shows a handful of peasants at work on it, trimming willows in spring, haying and harvesting wheat in summer, bringing home the cattle in fall, hunting and rollicking on the ice in winter—their lot linked to the changing seasons.

Bruegel was a pioneer in a number of ways. He gave free rein to what was, for his religion-ridden age, a notably avant-garde pictorial passion— his concern for everyday realism. In this concern, for example, he practically originated genre painting, the characteristically Netherlandish

Before the classically oriented Italian Renaissance style swept Europe and led to a more uniform appearance, the Northern and Southern approaches to a rendering of the human body varied considerably. Above are Adam and Eve from Van Eyck's dazzling *Ghent Altarpiece,* completed in 1432. Van Eyck's nudes reveal the influence of the stark, linear sweep and inward emotion of earlier Gothic forms, but they also demonstrate his new interest in the direct observation of nature. Recognizably human figures like these, shown with all their imperfections—Eve's straggly hair, Adam's chapped hands—became the trademark of northern European art.

art form devoted to showing common folk amusing themselves in company. In Bruegel's time the painting of landscapes and seascapes for their own sakes was still an unappreciated facet of Flemish art. Jan van Eyck and a series of Bruegel's famous Flemish ancestors, as well as most of his contemporaries, used outdoor scenery in their work, but it appeared mainly in tiny patches glimpsed past sacred figures in Biblical scenes or portraits. Bruegel triumphantly carried it much further. He was not only the first major artist to paint large seascapes; he also elevated landscape painting to new prominence by painting full-scale oils that were entirely bereft of any Biblical excuse. The picture called *Hunters in the Snow (pages 182-183)* is one of the happy results. What has made this moving view of peasants and snowbound scenery world famous, however, is not its place in the evolution of art but its overwhelming truthfulness of atmosphere. Better than any other painter before or since, Bruegel conveys the mood of a Northern winter, which broods over the world, dwarfing the lives of the dark figures who briefly inhabit it.

The contrast between this crowning achievement of Northern art and the work of Bruegel's contemporaries in Italy could not be more striking. For most Italian masters, art was in many ways as far from everyday life as representational painting can be. Because they aimed to capture in art those few perfect, ideal forms, which—as Plato taught the ancient Greeks —first served the gods as models at the original creation, the Italians valued beauty, harmonious composition and mathematically perfect perspective over literal content in their paintings. Accordingly, much that was eccentric, gnarled or intense—that is, most of what we now believe lends life and art their fascinating individuality—had to be suppressed.

Variations in taste and fashion make it pointless to argue about the relative greatness of different schools of painting. But it is possible to have reservations about the effects of the lofty Renaissance art theories, which, while bringing new sweep and scope to painting, also became something close to esthetic dogma from the 16th until well into the 19th Century. In doing so they unhappily imposed upon, and limited, the aims of art everywhere, and for centuries led to judgments of many earlier painters that were both unfair and misleading. Among the first to suffer was the reputation of Northern art generally, including the beautiful and pious works of the great 15th Century Flemish masters who were Bruegel's illustrious predecessors. Working between 1420 and 1500 these men, including Jan van Eyck, Roger van der Weyden, the Master of Flémalle (now generally identified also as Robert Campin), Hans Memling, Hugo van der Goes and a half dozen others, had justly enjoyed a high reputation in Europe until well into the 16th Century. Then the steam-rollerish popularity of High Renaissance art and theory began to spread across Europe. The Renaissance came to be viewed as a brilliant bridge over which all Europe had to pass from medieval darkness toward the Age of Reason. The very term medieval was invented by the Renaissance to describe what it saw as a gloomy, empty period between the death of ancient Greek and Roman culture and its triumphant rebirth. Because the Middle Ages did linger in the North, it became the fashion to see Northern culture as backward, its artists as inferior.

Flemish use of perspective, it was pointed out, was determined more by rule of thumb than anything else and fell far short of Italian geometric exactitude. Flemish handling of the human figure too, far from being noble and stately, was sometimes downright grotesque. Flemish Virgins, notably those by the Master of Flémalle and Memling, were often dumpy-looking and pale as a poached fish. Hugh van der Goes's Eve, naked in the Garden of Eden, was plainly potbellied and stringy. Such things were entirely against Italian Renaissance principles. It was not long before the greatest artist and most powerful personality of the South, Michelangelo himself, was denigrating the Flemish fondness for chatty detail and for painting everyday things as they are. "Their painting," he observed in conversations recollected by the Portuguese artist Francesco da Hollanda, "is of stuffs, bricks, mortar, the grass of the fields, the shadows of trees . . . and little figures here and there. And all this, though it may appear good in some eyes, is in truth done without . . . symmetry or proportion."

The preachment of a creative genius of Michelangelo's breadth and forcefulness was bound to be overwhelming during Bruegel's century. Though he painted the ceiling of the Sistine Chapel more than a decade before Bruegel was born, Michelangelo lived and worked long enough to be a contemporary of the Flemish painter; he died in 1564, just five years before Bruegel. By the 1550s Michelangelo's influence on the Flemish painting world had made Italianate painting so fashionable that, for many of Bruegel's contemporaries, the ability to paint in the Italian style became almost a professional necessity. The best-known Flemish painter of the age, for instance, was not Bruegel, whom we now recognize as the one great Flemish artist of his time, but a fellow painter named Frans Floris. This was true—in part at least—because Floris, in his *Fall of the Rebel Angels,* had been able to turn out a massive picture full of heavily muscled figures who look as if they had been lifted bodily from Michelangelo's *Last Judgment* on the wall of the Sistine Chapel.

This distorted evaluation of Northern painting was to become an enduring part of our inheritance from the Renaissance; its effect lasted about three centuries. During the long period of its dominance, 15th Century Flemish painters, as well as many others, were pejoratively labeled "primitives"—to indicate that they were too unsophisticated or too unskilled to observe Italian rules of perspective and proportion.

The first international show of 15th Century Flemish masters did not take place until 1902, in Bruges, and it is only in this century that the term "primitive" has begun to be abandoned. Today the Flemish 15th Century stands out as a dazzling era in art history—marked by its broad range of subject and feeling, and by its affecting blend of holiness and homely detail. The names and accomplishments of the great Netherlandish painters read like a litany of excellence: Jan van Eyck, who robed his stately Virgins in sacred light but opened a Gothic archway onto the real world; Roger van der Weyden, who achieved a kind of psychological realism by using the strange, distorted poses of his saintly mourners to spell out eternal Christian regret at Christ's suffering on the Cross; the Master of Flémalle, who turned the Virgin Mary into a plump, moon-

The great Florentine master Masaccio foreshadowed the future of much European painting in idealized, dynamic figures like this Adam and Eve from his series of frescoes painted around 1427 in the Brancacci Chapel in the church of Santa Maria del Carmine in Florence. With their heightened emotion, their vivid sense of movement and dramatic mood, these figures—monumental in character—seem to stride off the wall on which they are painted. Quite different from the unheroic figures of Van Eyck *(opposite page),* Masaccio's Adam and Eve have a quality of stately nobility that was to become standard throughout Europe.

faced girl receiving the angel messenger not, as custom dictated, in a holy place or a medieval walled garden but in a middle-class living room.

These early masters set the course of Flemish art and established its limits. Moreover, it is they who are generally credited with developing a revolutionary art technique: oil painting. They, at any rate, were the first to perfect the use of pigments mixed with oil instead of with tempera—a mixture of water and egg yolk—preferred by medieval Italian painters. Oil permitted the use of successive layers of translucent paint over an opaque base so that the colors could glow through, giving the paintings a radiance, a gloss and nuances of color never before seen in art.

As the achievements of the Northern painters have gradually been restored to their proper position, we have come to realize that to the extent that their art resisted the monumental and harmonious standards of the South, it was not being backward but was, instead, bent on preserving something of its own—a strength, intensity and crotchety truthfulness that the Southern concern for form and beauty threatened to extinguish. This realization has come with the understanding that the flowering of the North was not just a laggard version of the Italian Renaissance, but something very different—a largely independent development that can fairly be called the Northern Renaissance.

In the light of this new perspective has come a recognition that the Northern masters painted as they did not from any lack of skill but from the insight that perceives that truth can sometimes be better conveyed by a pale, awkward figure than by a gloriously graceful one. The whole early Flemish and German painting tradition can finally be seen as an enduring artistic contribution based on a concern for details of everyday life and a somber view of man's condition that rose from a profoundly different temperament. That temperament and the art it produced were fundamentally related to the character of the people, the conditions of their life and even to the climate of their Northern world.

At first glance, the differences between the art forms of North and South seem more attributable to differences in fashion and to historical happenstance than to regional character. Medieval Italian painting, for instance, found its early expression in the form of large, sacred frescoes painted directly on the interior walls of churches. The figures in these frescoes were often painted life-sized so they could be seen by the congregation; they were treated massively—frequently in a rather broad, posterish manner. Flemish painting, on the other hand, began in miniature with the small, luminous illustrations in the French and Flemish Books of Hours commissioned by medieval nobles. These were combined calendars and prayer books whose page margins were often decorated with leaves, flowers and small animals, rendered in magnifying-glass detail. The calendars were illustrated with exquisite pictures of seasonal activities in which whole scenes—with peasants, nobles and a bit of landscape—were compressed into a space the size of a playing card.

Yet even in this question of what size paintings should be—apparently determined by chance events—the profound influences of climate and countryside on art made themselves felt. When the Flemish painters finally did begin to work on larger pictures, mostly religious paintings for churches, as a general rule neither their surfaces nor their scope was as large as in Italian art. Why? Because in Italy church windows were usually small, to keep out heat and light in a land often drenched with sunshine. Church interiors, consequently, had quantities of wall space. In the north of Europe, by contrast, intense heat and light are rare, and heavy snows are frequent. This is why Gothic church architecture there developed high pointed roofs that shed the weight of accumulating snow and vast windows that let in what light there was. At the time French and Flemish artists began turning to panel painting, Northern churches were skeletal stone frameworks, with tall windows replacing the walls. In short, the Northern practice of using stained glass rather than wall paintings as the main decoration for churches was in part due to the weather.

The effects of climate on human behavior do not stop with art. Although today we are uneasy with the thought—it seems somehow unscientific—there is a link between countryside and character, between temperament and temperature. The Mediterranean *is* a blue and tideless sea. Italy *is* a country of little snow and much sun, with many regions where gentle rolling hills and olive trees can lull man into thinking that nature is entirely benevolent. No Northerner could ever think so. In northern Europe the forests were black and full of wolves. The North Sea had seething tides, which, in Holland and Belgium, licked inland with hungry tongues. Winter could and did kill. For months life was shrouded in gloom, and men drew in upon themselves to weather it.

An intuitive grasp of the cumulative effect of such things led the 19th Century English critic John Ruskin, one of the earliest writers to praise "primitives" in art, to an explanation of the differences between Italian and Flemish painting. "While Fra Angelico prayed and wept in his olive shade," Ruskin wrote in 1860, "there was different work doing in the dank fields of Flanders—wild seas to be banked out; endless canals to be dug . . . ploughing and harrowing of the frosty clay; careful breeding of stout horses and fat cattle; close setting of brick walls against cold winds and snow; much hardening of hands and gross stoutening of bodies in all this; gross jovialities of harvest homes and Christmas feasts, which were to be the reward of it."

Work, wind and weather, as Ruskin saw, can gnarl the mind as well as roughen the body. Northern literature and art reflect this process. They also, again and again, bear witness to a profound Northern preoccupation with the grotesqueries of everyday life and an acute awareness of how far man falls short, not only in shape but in spirit, of anything like grace or bronzed perfection. Whereas the South often liked to think of man, and to paint him, as a potential saint and hero, the North tended to see him as an incorrigible sinner, continually anguished by how far this bumbling and salacious creature was from either meriting a place in heaven or following the example of Christ's life on earth.

This harsh pessimism about human nature was clearly reflected in the religious atmosphere of the North. It was not by chance that the Reformation, which split the Christian world, began there. It is true that early attempts to reform the increasingly lax and profligate attitudes of the Church occurred in the South. The gentle example of St. Francis of Assisi, for example, was assimilated into the Church and institutionalized in the formation of the Franciscan order. But it was in the North that perennial disgust with man and society, as well as fear of the devil, finally led to violent religious revolution against Catholic worldliness.

Martin Luther was German. So, in origin and speech, were nearly all the people of the Netherlands; long before Luther, men in the Low Countries had been stirred by a strong reformist ardor and had banded together into zealous religious sects. One such influential group was the Brothers of the Common Life, a teaching order that helped train the great scholarly reformer of the age, Erasmus of Rotterdam. Appalled by man's behavior both in and out of religious orders, the Brothers instilled a lesson that Erasmus in his own scholarly way was to preach all his life. Its essence: a Christian must try to act like Christ. The results of man's failure to do so were savagely portrayed in the late 1400s by the nightmarish paintings of another Netherlander, Hieronymus Bosch—who was followed by a host of imitators including Pieter Bruegel. By contrast, Pope Leo X, who reigned over the crumbling fortunes of the Roman Church until 1520, saw society in a sunnier, more sophisticated and perhaps more Southern way. "God gave us the papacy," he once observed. "Let us enjoy it."

Today we are accustomed to think of the Low Countries as a cracker-sized, not very consequential corner of the world—Belgium dotted with light industry; Holland a haven for tulips and windmills. It takes a leap of the imagination to reconstruct a most important historical fact about these countries: during the Renaissance and the Reformation, and long before, they included one of the two great centers of European commerce and culture. One lay in Italy, with its handful of rich and powerful city-states. The other was the Netherlands, particularly Flanders, which sustained four powerful cities—Bruges, Ghent, Antwerp and Brussels.

Modern Bruges is a quaint little town with a quiet, meandering river,

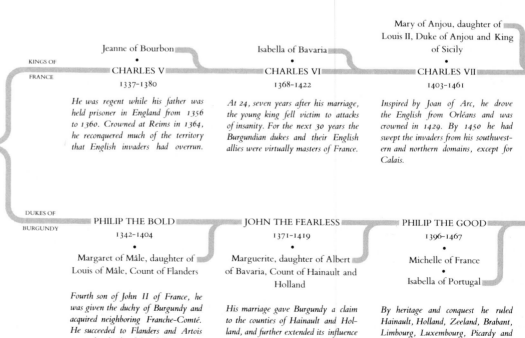

THROUGH MARRIAGE,
PURCHASE AND CONQUEST,
TWO BRANCHES OF THE VALOIS LINE
BUILT THE KINGDOM OF FRANCE
AND THE SPANISH EMPIRE

JOHN II, KING OF FRANCE
1319-1364
(son of Jeanne of Burgundy)
•
Bona of Luxembourg, daughter
of the King of Bohemia

KINGS OF FRANCE

Jeanne of Bourbon
•
CHARLES V
1337-1380

He was regent while his father was held prisoner in England from 1356 to 1360. Crowned at Reims in 1364, he reconquered much of the territory that English invaders had overrun.

Isabella of Bavaria
•
CHARLES VI
1368-1422

At 24, seven years after his marriage, the young king fell victim to attacks of insanity. For the next 30 years the Burgundian dukes and their English allies were virtually masters of France.

Mary of Anjou, daughter of
Louis II, Duke of Anjou and King
of Sicily
•
CHARLES VII
1403-1461

Inspired by Joan of Arc, he drove the English from Orléans and was crowned in 1429. By 1450 he had swept the invaders from his southwestern and northern domains, except for Calais.

DUKES OF BURGUNDY

PHILIP THE BOLD
1342-1404
•
Margaret of Mâle, daughter of
Louis of Mâle, Count of Flanders

Fourth son of John II of France, he was given the duchy of Burgundy and acquired neighboring Franche-Comté. He succeeded to Flanders and Artois upon the death of his father-in-law.

JOHN THE FEARLESS
1371-1419
•
Marguerite, daughter of Albert
of Bavaria, Count of Hainault and
Holland

His marriage gave Burgundy a claim to the counties of Hainault and Holland, and further extended its influence in the north. As regent for Charles VI, he had great power in France.

PHILIP THE GOOD
1396-1467
•
Michelle of France
•
Isabella of Portugal

By heritage and conquest he ruled Hainault, Holland, Zeeland, Brabant, Limbourg, Luxembourg, Picardy and Namur. During his long rule his lands were the most prosperous in Europe.

the Reye, and a fabulous picture gallery. It began as a trading center populated by descendants of Sixth Century Germans who migrated to the Netherlands to settle down and grow rich and independent on trade in fish and tin, wool and woven cloth, cattle and, eventually, art. By the 1100s Bruges had become a powerful autonomous city, which raised its own troops for defense and levied its own taxes. In fact, Bruges and its sister cities were the Northern equivalents of the Italian city-states. Thirteenth Century Bruges was stronger and richer than Paris. The same importance and prosperity touched Ghent, Brussels and Antwerp in succession. By the time of Pieter Bruegel's birth, the trade of Ghent and Bruges had begun to drop off as their river links to the sea slowly silted up, but Antwerp was on its way to becoming the richest trading city in the world, while in nearby Brussels a palace served as a home base for the Holy Roman Emperor, nominal ruler of more than half of Europe.

The creation of a great age in art, like the invention and manufacture of an atomic bomb, seems to require vast supplies of manpower and money. The Flemish cities, through their flourishing trade, had accumulated enough of both to nourish a brilliant artistic flowering. Not surprisingly, the nature of the art of that great age was strongly influenced by the international nature of the business. From England, from Hanseatic ports on the Baltic, from Scandinavia, Germany, France, Portugal, Spain and the whole Mediterranean world, goods and merchants streamed to the Low Countries. Over the centuries this cosmopolitan current showed itself in many cultural ways. In the 15th Century it brought fat Italian commissions to famous Flemish painters—Jan van Eyck, hired as early as 1434 by the rich trader Giovanni Arnolfini to paint a marriage portrait, which also served as an illustrated marriage certificate (pages 32-33); Hugo van der Goes, who was commissioned in 1475 by the Florentine merchant Tommaso Portinari to present the Portinari family as minor personages at the Nativity (pages 36-37). In the 16th

Charlotte, daughter of the
Duke of Savoy
•
Margaret, daughter of
James I of Scotland
•
LOUIS XI
1423-1483

*marrying Charlotte he opened a
[] to Italy. First overcoming Charles
Bold, he destroyed the great
[] es' power, unifying all France,
pt Brittany, under his absolute*

Anne, widow of
Francis I, Duke of Brittany
•
CHARLES VIII
1470-1498

*A weakling king, he nevertheless en-
larged the French realm through his
negotiated marriage with the Duchess
of Brittany. He died without heirs,
succeeded by Louis of Orléans.*

SPANISH
HABSBURGS

Maximilian I of Habsburg,
King of Germany, Holy Roman Emperor
1459-1519

CHARLES THE BOLD
1433-1477
•
Catherine of France
•
Isabella of Bourbon
•
Margaret, sister of
Edward IV of England

*[] ing and winning Alsace, Guelder
[] and Lorraine, Charles almost
[] ed his scattered fiefs into a new
[] gdom. His daring dream died with
[] on the battlefield before Nancy.*

MARY OF BURGUNDY
(last of Burgundian line)
1457-1482

*Though Louis XI took Burgundy
proper, she retained the north Burgundian lands of Flanders, Artois, Holland, Franche-Comté, Zeeland, Luxembourg, Namur, Brabant, Hainault
and Limbourg.*

PHILIP I OF SPAIN
(called "the Handsome")
1478-1506
•
Joanna the Mad, heiress of
the King of Spain

*Succeeding to his mother's Burgundian
domains in the north, he extended
them by conquering the duchy of
Friesland. His marriage brought him
the crowns of Castile and of Spain.*

**CHARLES V, HOLY ROMAN
EMPEROR**
(King of Spain, abdicated 1556)
1500-1558
•
Isabella of Portugal

*His reign saw his Netherlands territo-
ry extended, the duchy of Württem-
berg added to his Habsburg heritage,
and the acquisition of the golden lands
of Mexico and Peru for Spain.*

PHILIP II OF SPAIN
1527-1598
•
Maria of Portugal
•
Mary Tudor, Queen of England
•
Elizabeth of Valois
•
Anna, daughter of Maximilian II,
Holy Roman Emperor

*Ruler of his father's lands in Italy, the
Low Countries and Franche-Comté
by 1555, King of Spain and Spanish
America the next year, he made good
his maternal claim to the Portuguese
crown in 1581.*

Century the prestige of Flemish culture drew great foreign painters like Albrecht Dürer to Flanders and carried a Flemish peasant dance to Spain, where it took root and is still known by the Spanish word for Flemish—flamenco.

By Bruegel's time the foreign fancy for Flemish art, both old and new, had become prodigious. King Philip II of Spain filled the private rooms of the Escorial, his Renaissance palace near Madrid, with Bosch's images of sinners in action. He commissioned a full-scale copy of Van Eyck's *Ghent Altarpiece.* He installed a Utrecht portraitist and contemporary of Bruegel's, Antonis Mor, as court painter in Madrid. With his name conveniently changed to Antonio Moro, the artist did portraits of the whole Spanish royal family and even accompanied Philip to England to make a portrait of Mary Tudor, the King's sour-visaged bride-to-be.

Besides the prosperity of Flanders and its international flavor, there was still another factor that played an important part in setting the course of Flemish art. To understand it fully, it is necessary to turn back to one of those dynastic quirks that so often changed the course of European history. The chain of events that put Flanders into the forefront of European culture and ended by making the whole Netherlands the bitterly contested property of a foreign king began in France two centuries earlier. At Poitiers in 1356, in one of the early battles of the Hundred Years' War, a French king, John the Good, was defeated in battle by the English. John was kept prisoner, along with his youngest son, Philip the Bold, for a number of years. When he was finally released, King John, as a reward for his son's cheerfulness and courage in captivity, gave Philip a section of land in the vicinity of Dijon. Then, as now, it was called Burgundy.

Many a prince of the blood might have been content to sit back and enjoy the wine of the country. After all, it had a certain reputation, although it was not quite so admired by the nobles of the time as the sweet white wine of Cyprus. Philip, however, was not called "the Bold" for nothing, and his sons took after him. During the rest of the Hundred Years' War, for instance, in hopes of acquiring land and power, he and his heirs allied themselves first with the English, then with their cousins who were kings of France. Thereafter, with relentless ambition they fought and intermarried with everyone who had holdings in the Netherlands. One by one, through strategic efforts by the Dukes of Burgundy in boudoirs and on battlefields, the flourishing sections of the Netherlands—once the property of English lords, Habsburg princes and French nobles—fell under their control. Soon they had created a brand-new Burgundy: a wedge-shaped section of land as long as present-day West Germany and, in contemporary terms, far more powerful. It included all of what is now Holland and Belgium and most of the land—except Lorraine—lying southward between modern Belgium and the city of Dijon.

That sleepy provincial center, renowned now mainly for its mustard, was for decades the bustling capital of all Burgundy. The sprawling dukedom's trading wealth, however, was centered in the North. The Dukes spent much of the year in Flanders, built lavish palaces in Flemish cities and finally moved their court to Brussels. Most of their Northern subjects spoke German or German dialects and few, except the Walloons living around Liège, spoke French in any form. Yet the Dukes were able to introduce French as the language of the courts and the nobility. To help turn the Netherlands into a unified territory, they convened meetings of local powers from all over Burgundy, and they created a chivalric order, the Order of the Golden Fleece, which made the Northern nobles their trusted counselors and vassals.

Important as these steps were in the political unification of the Netherlands, the Dukes' most lasting impact on the area was cultural. For, accompanying the Burgundian appetite for power was a superlative taste in art, which the Dukes had the means to gratify. Like their cousins and neighbors the Dukes of Berry and the Valois kings of France, the Burgundians spent liberally to beautify their churches, their palaces, their books, altarpieces and tombs.

The result was that more than a hundred years before the art of the Italian Renaissance was to sweep triumphantly northward in the 16th Century and overwhelm "backward" Flanders, the Dukes of Burgundy had brought together in their courts all the elements needed to create a dazzling flowering of Northern art. In the fruitfulness of their court painters we now recognize the first strong stirrings of the Northern Renaissance.

One source of this Burgundian interest in art was the ducal delight in small, beautifully wrought objects and in lavish chivalric display. To satisfy these tastes they hired goldsmiths and sculptors who shaped from gold and silver, limestone and wood a succession of priceless objects—intricate containers for sacred relics, rich seals and clasps and even artful salt cellars—on most of which appeared carved lions, lambs and flowers, saints, beggars and cripples and the likenesses of the Dukes themselves. The gilded richness and brilliant colors of this artistry were carried over into illustrations for the Books of Hours, which the Dukes also commissioned by the dozens.

The Dukes of Burgundy were conspicuously openhanded. On one oc-

A masterpiece of miniature painting, the Book of Hours of the Flemish Duchess Catherine of Cleves is one of the finest examples of an art form that was brought to perfection by late 14th and 15th Century artists of northern Europe. The Books of Hours, which combined prayers and a calendar, were illuminated by religious scenes, glimpses of landscape and pious fantasies. The unknown artist of this work shows, in the two pages reproduced at the left, Catherine kneeling before the Madonna and Child (*far left*) and, with perhaps a more vivid imagination, scenes of the damned being goaded into the mouth of hell.

casion the court hired the entire membership of the painting guilds in at least 12 Netherlandish cities and kept them busy for weeks creating decorations for the wedding of Charles the Bold with Margaret of York in 1468. (Among other things, this army of Flemish artists and artisans fashioned a perfect model whale with 40 people inside it and a Gothic tower, 46 feet high, which served as a centerpiece for the banquet table.) Inevitably, such largess brought artists flocking to the great art centers of the North. Many were Flemings, like Roger van der Weyden and Jan van Eyck; many came from northern Italy.

The Italian artists brought with them a sweeping style, an awareness of space and distance, an interest in softly modeled human figures, which Northern painters and sculptors, still confined to book illustrations and precious objects, must have found new and exhilarating. Book illustrations began to include stretches of country landscape. And when Northern painters turned to larger panel paintings, as they soon did, they created an art that increasingly combined the best of everything: the Burgundian gemlike decoration, the Flemish passion for realistic detail, the softer lines and wider spaces hinted at by the Italians. This graceful blend has come to be known as the International style.

Carried further and brilliantly transformed, the elements of this style served as a base for the work of Van Eyck and his followers. The most monumental early landmarks in this newly established tradition include the Master of Flémalle's *Merode Altarpiece* of 1425-1428, Van Eyck's *Ghent Altarpiece* of 1432 and Roger van der Weyden's *Descent from the Cross*, c. 1435 (*pages 34-35*). It is here that Van der Weyden's anguished mourners reveal their emotional state through tormented poses. The Master of Flémalle's Virgin, hearing the Annunciation from the Archangel Gabriel while seated among cooking pots, fire irons and patched floor boards, sanctifies in art the ineradicable Flemish penchant for depicting the things of daily life, even in scenes of high sacredness. Van Eyck's multipaneled altarpiece shows a triple debt to the past: he preserves the Burgundian passion for jewelry by dressing his saintly choristers in gem-encrusted robes; he expresses his interest in landscape by opening up the central panel of the altarpiece onto a spring countryside; and, true to the tradition of the Books of Hours, he reveals every leaf and flower in precise and delicate detail.

At the height of Burgundian power in 1475, Charles the Bold, the last great Duke of Burgundy, controlled an irregular area of land (*shaded*) extending more than 500 miles from the Alps in the south to the shores of the North Sea. Today those former domains comprise the kingdoms of Belgium and the Netherlands, the grand duchy of Luxembourg and parts of France and West Germany.

With the death in 1477 of the last and most ambitious duke, Charles the Bold, the Burgundian era ended, and a new, even more important but not quite so happy age in Netherlandish history began. Burgundy was split in two. The French King swiftly engulfed the area around Dijon. Charles had arranged the marriage of his only child, a daughter, to a Habsburg, and so the northern territories, including Brussels, became part of the vast holdings of that tenacious and far-flung family, which was to hold a dominant position in Europe for several more centuries.

Even if flourishing international trade had not been enough to guarantee that the Low Countries would continue to find themselves at the cosmopolitan heart of Europe during the 16th Century, the presence in Brussels of the court of the Holy Roman Emperor would have done so. That Emperor was Charles V, a Habsburg prince born in Ghent in the year 1500. Both in his person and in the forces that he chose to fight throughout his reign, Charles proved one of the most tragically heroic figures of his age. And it was he who, more than any other, helped shape the political world of Pieter Bruegel's early years.

By the 16th Century the final breakup of the feudal system had created a need for rulers to exercise personal power in its place. As a result Charles's century became an age of great national kings, claiming to govern by divine right and practicing politics with towering international ambition. We know them well enough from history books: Henry VIII, who led England away from the Church of Rome in 1534; Charles V's own son, Philip II of Spain, the spearhead of the Catholic Counter Reformation; Elizabeth, Henry's daughter and Philip's sister-in-law, who gave her name to an age; Francis I, whose one-track Gallic ambition to make France and Francis first in Europe was a continual threat to everyone.

Charles was linked by blood to nearly everybody (including, rumor said, Julius Caesar) who had ever been anybody in European history. From his Habsburg father, Philip the Fair, and his Spanish mother, Joanna of Castile, he inherited not only most of Spain but also much of Italy and all of the Netherlands. Under normal circumstances he might have entered the company of his fellow kings as just one more land-hungry monarch trying to consolidate or expand his realms. Indeed, much of his life was devoted to such maneuverings, and to a long duel with Francis for supremacy in Europe. But in 1519, thanks to quantities of borrowed money and the connections of his Austrian Habsburg cousins, Charles was elected Holy Roman Emperor. The job brought with it, at least for Charles, a different international role and a special sense of responsibility for the protection of Christian Europe.

Charles often appears to us in portraits by his many court painters as an energetic-looking soldier. His armor is shiny, his protruding chin and neatly cropped beard under an arched beaky nose look formidable indeed. But for all his arrogant bearing, Charles was a modest and devout person and a man brought up to prize chivalric honor as it had been practiced in the courts of Burgundy in the time of his great grandfather, Charles the Bold. If the new Emperor was far from brilliant, he worked hard, knew his limitations and listened to his advisers. He strove continually to understand 16th Century Europe and what was happening to it, and there is no way of knowing whether or not, as he poured out his life and wealth defending the Holy Roman Empire, he realized that whatever he did, it was doomed.

At any rate, Charles was the last Emperor to take the job seriously. The fact is a measure of his devotion to duty and of his adherence to the medieval concept that a man's politics and his religion are inseparable. It is also a measure of the Empire's decay. First created in the 10th Century as an artificial restoration of Charlemagne's domains, it had been the embodiment of the medieval idea of a universal empire, in which all of Catholic Christendom was seen as a viable political structure to be guarded by a watchdog Emperor who would protect it, in God's name, from outer threat and inner schism. But the Empire had been in steady decline since the 1200s, and by Charles's time it had not so much outlived its use-

By Bruegel's day in 1556, the vast holdings once controlled by Charles the Bold (*shaded areas, opposite page*) had passed to Spain's Philip II, Charles's great-great-grandson. But those territories had been considerably reduced to the shaded areas on the map above. Picardy, Burgundy proper and parts of Groningen had been seized by neighboring France and Germany; Lorraine won independence.

fulness as it had outlived its capacity to stay alive at all.

Charles's election as Emperor did not assure him of an unchallenged position as ruler of Christian Europe. The Empire was seriously divided internally by national ambitions and by the growing controversy over the corruption of the Catholic Church. Moreover the Church itself added to the trouble by acting as an independent spiritual and temporal power that frequently regarded the Holy Roman Emperor as just one more ambitious prince. During Charles's reign one Pope signed a treaty with Francis against Charles and another withdrew his armies from Charles's support in a war with the German Protestant princes. Charles could not even count on total support from his fellow Christian monarchs to defend Europe against the forces of Suleiman the Magnificent, the Turkish sultan who boasted that he would overrun Europe and stable his horses in St. Peter's.

Suleiman was the bogeyman of the Christian world. He threatened the Empire through most of Charles's lifetime and often seemed its most formidable danger. But, though the Turks remained a sea power until 1571, Charles helped check their armies at the gates of Vienna in 1529, and in 1535 he uprooted their foothold in North Africa by invading Tunis. In the long run it proved to be the inner pressures and national rivalries and above all the schism in the Church that defeated Charles and fragmented the Empire.

From 1519 until 1555 Charles vainly strove to keep Martin Luther's Protestant rebellion from proliferating into even more outrageous heresies—like the Anabaptist call to abolish all private property in the name of Christian charity. At the same time he labored mightily to keep responsible reformers and irate orthodox Catholics negotiating within the framework of the Church. It was Charles who urged the Pope to call the Council of Trent, an assembly of prelates who met on and off for 18 years (from 1545 to 1563) trying to decide, with little success, what degree of deviation could be countenanced within the Church. Charles's troops lent muscle to the Counter Reformation, a movement intended to make the Church Militant both more militant and more attractive. These steps were sound, but ultimately they failed. The schism was not healed. The Protestant Reformation was not stifled. The fortunes of the Empire dwindled steadily.

To raise operating expenses, Charles borrowed vast sums of money from bankers, particularly the incredibly wealthy Fugger family of Augsburg. Furthermore, he was continuously entangled in Imperial rivalries. He could not put real pressure on the German princes to restrain the Protestants in their domains, because he often needed them to help fight the Turks. Besides, they resented any interference in their interior affairs by a Habsburg prince, however imperial his title or universal his aims. An even greater stumbling block was Francis I of France. Francis had desperately wanted to be elected Holy Roman Emperor himself, and when he lost he became Charles's implacable enemy. Though a Catholic, Francis did not scruple to take advantage of Charles's wars on behalf of Christendom to send French soldiers into Catholic Italy. He even went so far as to form an alliance with the Turks against Charles. Once, acting in the proudest chivalric tradition, Charles offered to fight him in single combat with their crowns at stake, but nothing ever came of it.

It was a crowning irony of Charles's life that, as the years advanced and the bitter enmity between the Protestant sects and the Catholic establishment grew cancerously in his own home territory, the Netherlands, he was helpless to stop it. Actually, the situation never did quite get out of hand during his lifetime. Charles was popular in the Netherlands; until his death Netherlanders looked upon their country as the center of Charles's Empire. Again and again they provided him with gold, troops and even good generals of noble blood to fight Francis. Charles could not know that within a decade of his death many of these same nobles would rebel against his son Philip to give Catholic Europe and its Counter Reformation the most decisive reverse they would jointly suffer.

It was from Brussels that Charles had first set out to preserve the Empire. It was to Brussels that he returned in 1555, old before his time, suffering from gout and all but bankrupt, to lay down his impossible burden. He abdicated his powers and only three years later died—after playing a last diplomatic card, the arrangement of a marriage between his son and Mary Tudor, then the violently Catholic Queen of England. Their son, Charles reasoned with traditional dynastic logic, would be brought up a Catholic and reverse the heresy of Henry VIII, thus ensuring that England would remain in the ranks of Catholic Christendom.

That Mary proved barren (as well as ugly) was not really Charles's fault. Nor, in the light of history, can he be blamed for failing to perpetuate an Empire already moribund when he inherited it. But it is clear that he was guilty of a profound failure to grasp the nature of the underlying forces working against him: the spread of Renaissance learning and vernacular literature, which helped undermine the authority of the Church among the people; Protestant zeal and a new spirit of nationalism, which combined to resist the old Imperial political ideal.

Charles left the remnants of his Imperial power to his Austrian brother Ferdinand, and entrusted Spain and the Netherlands to his son Philip—whose succession was to have tragic consequences for the Low Countries. Philip was a Spaniard by birth, training and lifelong residence, and a far more fanatical Catholic than his father. (It was not by chance that the painter El Greco, thinking to create a picture to please Philip and so win himself a court job, produced a fiery view of a whalelike hell mouth swallowing sinners and called it "Philip's Dream.") To Netherlanders in Bruegel's time, Flemish-born Charles had seemed as natural as the sun, a revered part of their world—powerful, radiant and only occasionally frightening. But Philip was a foreigner. He stayed in far-off Madrid, meticulously and cruelly working to expunge all Protestantism from the Low Countries. Within a decade he had driven into open rebellion thousands of Netherlandish leaders who had been loyal to his father, and created a bitter national resentment against himself and against Spain.

Pieter Bruegel was 30 when Philip began his disastrous rule. During the troubled years that followed he painted some of his finest pictures. The torment that wracked the Netherlands during those years shaped his maturity and lent somber substance to his work.

The Flemish Masters

In the early 15th Century, at the beginning of the Italian Renaissance, another great era in art was born in the Low Countries. It was spurred into being by the rise of a handful of rich, trading cities, mainly in Flanders, and nourished by a generous, art-minded aristocracy and a newly affluent middle class of burghers and bankers. Like most art, then and for generations, Flemish painting was rooted in medieval religion and largely devoted to scenes from the life of Christ and the saints. But the artists of the time treated the objects in their symbol-filled pictures with a vigorous new delight in their tangible reality—in the weight, texture and color of the natural world. To aid them, they developed an old and little-used medium—oil painting— to a dazzling perfection. Capturing brilliant effects of light and atmosphere with their luminous colors, the Flemish masters brought new life to the landscape backgrounds of their religious works—some of the most moving paintings known—and created a body of meticulous portraits, which are unsurpassed in objectivity and psychological penetration.

But their unique contribution, one that has caused their work to last these many centuries, was in being able to demonstrate in art their profound conviction that all the little details of everyday life—from a glimpse through a window to the glint of sunlight on a jewel—are charged with beauty and meaning.

Like much Northern art, Flemish oil painting had its origins in medieval manuscript illumination. The link is clearly shown in this page-sized oil panel, reproduced actual size. Precise in every detail— gleaming glass, dull metal, nappy wool—it shows St. Jerome, guarded by a lion, reading in his study.

Jan van Eyck: *St. Jerome in His Study*, 1441

Few subjects were treated more often by Flemish painters, or with more religious and artistic devotion, than the Madonna and Child. But the pious images that resulted—as these two paintings show—varied enormously. Below, Mary appears as a robust burgher's wife, holding her long-limbed Infant in a comfortable bourgeois living room, with a handsome, wicker firescreen suggesting her halo and a window opening on a crisp view of a Flemish town. The picture is attributed to the anonymous Master of Flémalle, whom many scholars believe to be Robert Campin. It has a homey, down-to-earth quality that would have appealed to a middle-class owner's materialistic tastes. Yet the artist

has skillfully blended everyday reality with familiar spiritual symbols—from the chalice, which the Baby Jesus would one day use at the Last Supper, to a plain, three-legged stool, which stands for the Trinity. In contrast, Jan van Eyck pictured the Virgin as the Queen of Heaven in an ornate cathedral setting. Seated between vari-colored marble columns surmounted by sculptured Apostles, she is enthroned on a rich Oriental rug beneath an elegant canopy. In all these things Van Eyck, who was a protégé of the Dukes of Burgundy, reveals his patrons' aristocratic tastes as well as his own sheer delight and rare skill in recreating the scintillating surfaces of precious things.

Master of Flémalle: *Virgin and Child Before a Firescreen*, 1420–1425

Jan van Eyck: *Madonna* (central panel of a triptych), 1432-1433

31

Jan van Eyck: *The Marriage of Giovanni Arnolfini and Jeanne Cenami*, 1434

In 1434 Jan van Eyck painted one of the most remarkable wedding portraits in all art. Its subject is Van Eyck's friend, Giovanni Arnolfini, a prosperous Bruges merchant, exchanging vows with his bride. In those days—and, indeed, until 1563 when the Church began to require a priestly witness—it was proper to marry simply by swearing private vows. But Arnolfini, being a man of substance, evidently felt the need not only for a beautiful souvenir, but for witnesses as well. Accordingly, in his

painting Van Eyck inscribed *Johannes de Eyck fuit hic* (Jan van Eyck was here) on the wall *(opposite)* and showed reflections of himself and another man in the convex mirror. Like the ceremony itself, the picture unites flesh and spirit. Many realistic details are also religious symbols: the lone candle signifying the all-seeing Christ's presence, the small dog representing fidelity and the abandoned slippers revealing that the couple is standing upon holy ground, inside the marriage bedroom.

Roger van der Weyden was a newly accredited master in 1435 when he received a handsome commission from the Louvain Archers' Guild to paint a triptych altarpiece for their local church. This intensely moving *Descent from the Cross* is the central panel from that work; the wings have been lost.

Though still young in his art, Van der Weyden accomplished two remarkable things in this large picture—it is over eight feet across. He compressed the emotion so that the scene seems charged with electric tension, yet he maintained a dignified restraint that keeps it from being maudlin or histrionic.

The emotion of the panel is centered on the body of the dead Christ and the figure of His mother. Fainting with grief, Mary has slumped to the ground in a posture that echoes that of her Son, drooping in the arms of Joseph of Arimathea and Nicodemus. The sympathetic connection between them is further enhanced by the fall of Jesus' pierced hand, which almost touches His mother's.

Even a brief analysis of the painting's disciplined composition will show how Van der Weyden focused attention on his drama. Two figures, St. John stooping to assist the Virgin and the hand-wringing Mary Magdalen opposite, bracket the action like parentheses. The artist suppressed nearly all the usual symbolic paraphernalia, reducing the scene to its essentials; the Cross itself is almost hidden, the skull—a traditional reminder that the setting was Golgotha, where Adam was buried—appears as a mere footnote. No distant landscape relieves the viewer's concentration on the passion of the mourners. Everything is enclosed in a gilded niche, a kind of shallow stage. And within this frame, it is the emotion on believably human faces and the expressive, sculptural poses of grieving limbs that eloquently tell the tale.

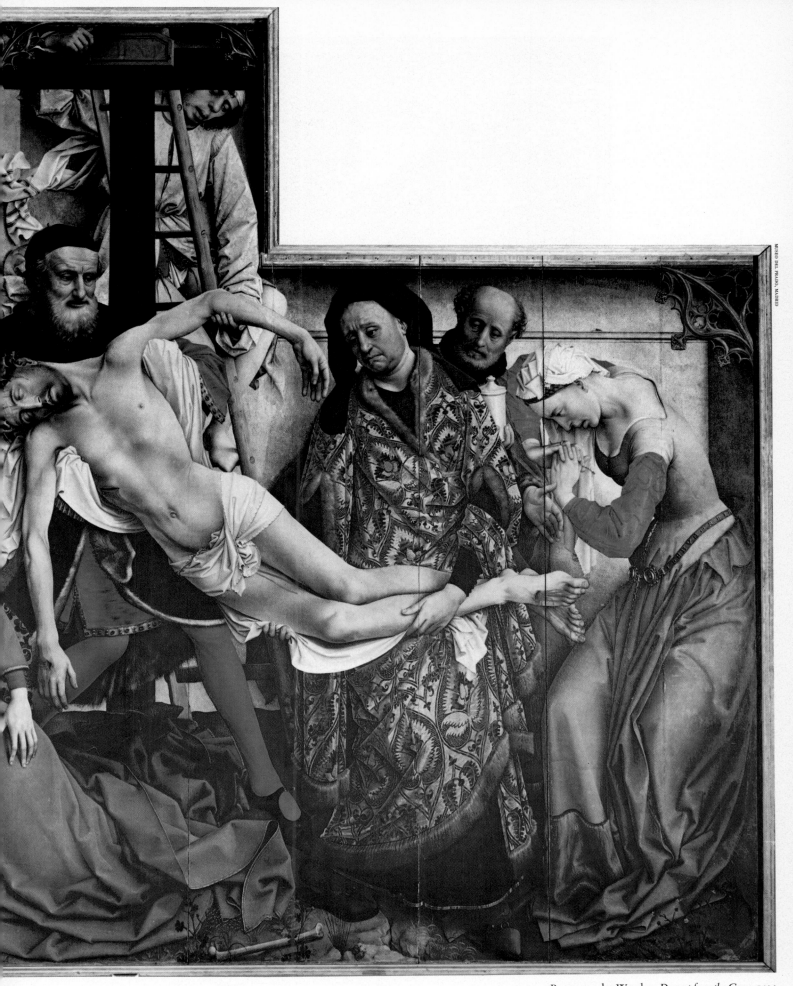

Roger van der Weyden: *Descent from the Cross*, 1435

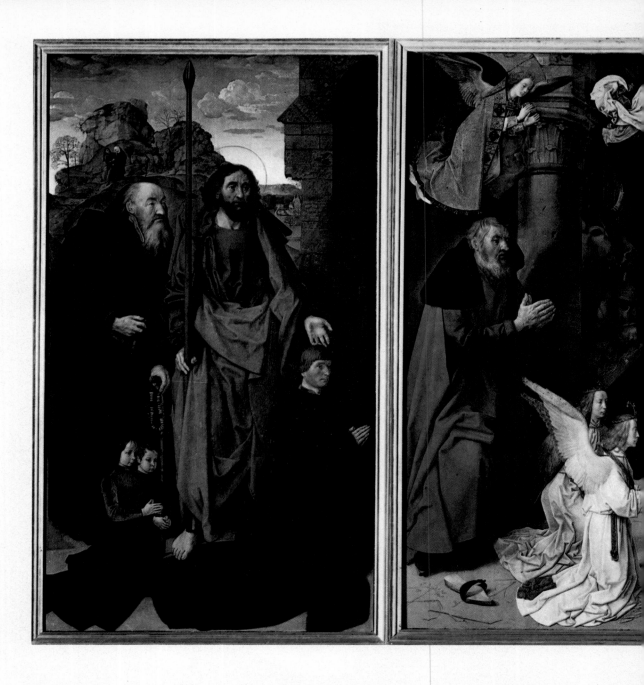

Working in Bruges more than a generation after the death of Jan van Eyck, Hugo van der Goes painted this brilliant, monumental triptych—the central panel alone is 10 feet across. In many ways, the painting sums up the best elements of the Flemish tradition —its cool, natural color, its lifelike portraiture, symbolic details and the tiny, storytelling, narrative scenes in the distant landscape. The small figures in the left-hand panel are Mary and Joseph approaching Bethlehem; the center reveals shepherds joyfully dancing at the news of Christ's birth and the right panel depicts the approach of the Magi. Van der Goes painted it for an Italian, Tommaso Portinari, a wealthy agent of the Medici in Bruges, who commissioned it for his family chapel in Florence. In keeping with custom, Van der Goes included donor Portinari kneeling with his two sons in the left panel and his wife and daughter in the right panel. And, as tradition dictated, he made them smaller than their patron saints behind them. But Van der Goes was an innovator as well as a distinguished follower. Into the meditative mood of the central panel he has thrust three work-worn shepherds, pictured fully as large as the Madonna and Joseph. These rough Flemish men, their simple reverence contrasting sharply with the cool elegance of the saints, provide a fresh breath of realism in the painting of religious scenes and foreshadow the plain folk and human vitality of the world of Bruegel.

Hugo van der Goes: *Adoration of the Shepherds with Saints and Donors (Portinari Altarpiece)*, c.1476

Jan van Eyck: *Man in a Red Turban* (self-portrait?), 1433

Squinting slightly—perhaps from having stared long into a mirror—the man gazing confidently out of the picture above may be Van Eyck himself. Van der Weyden's young lady's demurely downcast eyes belie the sensuality of her pouting lower lip. In masterful paintings like these, using the revealing three-quarter view they invented— profiles had been the norm—Flemish artists created portraits of unmatched objectivity and rare beauty.

Roger van der Weyden: *Portrait of a Lady*, 1455-1460

39

II

Giving the Devil His Due

Everybody knows that hell would be a fine place to visit. But nowadays
nobody seriously considers having to live there. This was not always the
case. For the Flemish citizen of the 16th Century, hell was as real (one
chronicler explained) as a sore tooth. The devil, it followed, was a public
personage, much more fearful and a great deal more powerful than, say,
Attila the Hun.

Man's position regarding sin and retribution had been clearly stated
by the early Church. When the trumpets sounded at the Last Judgment
and the numberless infinities of dead rose from their graves, clad, as custom decreed, only in their innocence, all those judged guilty of mortal
sin would go straight to hell forever. Those guilty of venial sins would
go to purgatory for temporary torment. A happy handful of the truly innocent would go to heaven where, according to St. John, God would
wipe the tears forever from their eyes.

Such conceptions did not begin to fade with the new learning intro-
duced by the Renaissance. Fear of the devil and concern with the
machinery of punishment and salvation, in fact, grew more intense during the Reformation and long after, for men felt themselves made
vulnerable by the decline of the Catholic Church and by the evident
progress of iniquity in a world where the old order and unquestioning
faith were both crumbling away. Accordingly, well into Pieter Bruegel's
lifetime it remained the fashion for the fearful and the faithful alike to
meditate upon, write about and paint what were known as The Four Last
Things: Death, the Last Judgment, Heaven and Hell.

For painters and writers, heaven as a subject proved almost a total loss.
Near its blue vault the air grows thin; the presumptuous creative imagination falters. A sense of sacrilege sets in, and the artist, especially the
devout artist, is likely to have difficulty with the job of description, as
even Dante did in the third book of the *Divine Comedy,* where he ram-
bles on about eternal harmony and light. But hell and the devil have
always been more rewarding subjects. Dante, for instance, livened up
the *Inferno* by putting all his personal and political enemies there
and by making the devil's punishments fit their crimes: flatterers were

dipped in excrement; sowers of schism in the Church were themselves made literally schismatic by little devils wielding sharp, dissecting knives. The preoccupation with defining and describing hell has remained popular until today, although infernal conceptions have grown more and more sophisticated. A notable recent attempt, by Jean-Paul Sartre, playwright-priest of French Existentialism, rejected the idea that the inferno is a nether region. "Hell," Sartre preached instead, in his play *No Exit,* "is other people."

Yet of all the master painters and poets who have tried to give the devil and his works their due in the centuries since Dante, no one has ever quite matched a mysterious, brilliant and apparently pious predecessor of Bruegel's, a Netherlander named Hieronymus Bosch. A haggard, glittery-eyed man—at least so he appears in a sketched portrait presumed to be of him—Bosch was born in the Brabant town of 's Hertogenbosch about 1450 and died there in 1516, already recognized as one of the unforgettable artists of his or any other age.

Bosch was to diabolic painting approximately what Henry Ford became to the automobile. He didn't invent it, but after he got involved the product was never the same again—and his name has been inseparably linked with it ever since. *Last Judgments* there had been in plenty, but never on so fearful a scale as Bosch's, with a whole menagerie of petty monsters turned loose upon surrealistic landscapes to scarify sinners. With chilling effect Bosch preached morality by painting the painful torments in store for sinners in hell, and he was equally adept at depicting the horrible cruelty and ugliness of men doing the devil's work here on earth. Sometimes, at least to judge from figures in his paintings that are thought to resemble him, he democratically included himself in both unpleasant categories. It was the Northern tradition in paintings of the Passion to make Christ's tormentors both angry and ugly. But until Bosch's paintings, like the *Carrying of the Cross (page 59),* no one had ever seen such an assortment of pie-faced, snaggle-toothed, wart-nosed human beings thronging around St. Veronica or crowding against the preternaturally passive Christ figure as He is jostled along the way to Calvary.

Bosch, in fact, seems to have been haunted by the mindless cruelty of human beings and the fascinating, ferretlike vitality of true ugliness. Yet by some stroke of psychological genius, in depicting men he never quite pushes his outrageous caricatures beyond the frontier of credibility. Even his sadistic monsters sometimes seem troublingly human. As a result, Bosch shows better than any painter how men in crowds wavering toward violence are taken by a kind of seizure, like epilepsy, which spreads from eye to eye, from hand to hand. A kind of temporary insanity— sometimes incited merely by the sheer vulnerability of the victim—sits on their sweating faces, still shaped in the likeness of a human individuality they have temporarily shed. It can be seen in one version of *Ecce Homo* by Bosch in the worried look of a merchant who is realizing that the Crucifixion will not be good for business; and in the frail, squirrel-eyed old man with a billy-goat beard in *The Crowning with Thorns (page 40)* who pats Jesus' soon-to-be-tortured flesh in anticipation, like a marketing housewife pinching chickens to check for plumpness.

This portrait of Hieronymus Bosch, whose paintings greatly influenced Bruegel, is one of three presumed likenesses that still survive. It is thought to be a copy of a self-portrait Bosch did near the end of his life. Though it shows him as an old man, the impression of age conveyed by his deeply furrowed face and stringy neck is belied by the intensity of his piercing gaze.

Bosch's nightmarish demons and hellish wastelands have had their effect on nearly all the terrifying and surrealist art that followed him, from the *Witches' Sabbath* and the dark, fantastic *Los Caprichos* of Goya to Dali's strange Martian landscapes. The gross and degenerate human forms and faces in Bosch's paintings find echoes in the works of many later satirists —William Hogarth, for instance, exposing the debaucheries of 18th Century London with savage laughter. Bosch's closest link with later artists and audiences, though, was forged by Pieter Bruegel. Of all the painters, Flemish and otherwise, whom Bruegel had to assimilate before he really became Bruegel, none had more apparent influence on him— or proved less digestible—than Hieronymus Bosch.

Their relationship, in fact, is hardly paralleled in art. Bruegel grew to be a greater painter than Bosch in range, sustained power and humanity. In the process, like every genius, he borrowed and made entirely his own, themes and details garnered from all over the art world—from Jan van Eyck's religious paintings, from the global landscapes of an early 16th Century master called Joachim Patinir, from Michelangelo's frescos in the Sistine Chapel. It sometimes takes an expert eye, however, to mark these traces in his work. But Bosch's influence on a major segment of Bruegel's paintings and drawings is so evident that the earlier painter sometimes seems to have been swallowed whole into the body of Bruegel's work, his outline clearly visible and identifiable, like an undigested goat in the elastic stomach of a python.

Inexperienced art viewers who come upon Bosch first and then encounter Bruegel's *Dulle Griet (Mad Meg) (pages 66-67),* a picture that shows a giantess storming hell at the head of a troop of old women and includes a swarm of hybrid monsters and a fiercely fanged hell mouth, invariably think it is by Bosch. The confusion is not confined to amateurs. Until the turn of the century even the experts differed sharply about which man painted which pictures.

Bosch, of course, is a painter whose influence it would be hard for another painter to hide. But the fact is that Bruegel, when he began drawing and painting like Bosch—probably at the command of his employer in Antwerp—had no wish to disguise his sources. For though Bosch died about 10 years before Bruegel was born, his paintings were still enjoying an enormous vogue nearly a half century later, when Bruegel was beginning to find his stride as an artist in the Antwerp of the 1550s. Twelve copies of Bosch's *Temptation of St. Anthony (pages 64-65)* were in circulation at that time—some made by Bosch himself, others done under his supervision in his workshop, still others done by later painters on commission. When Bruegel began borrowing from Bosch, he was not simply picking up small tricks to enrich his own style. He was consciously aping the work of a famous artist in order to make money.

Still, Bosch's diabolical preoccupations and searing caricatures clearly appealed to Bruegel personally as well as professionally, just as they appealed to the tastes of Bruegel's age in general. The passionate preachment against human folly and the almost pathological fear of the devil, which lingered in northern Europe long after we like to think the benign light of humanism and Renaissance learning had banished them to the shadowy corners of civilization, were partly responsible for Bosch's appeal. Yet the painter clearly evokes a response that is not limited to a given age. It is striking how provocative Bosch's diabolism seems even in our own century, which thinks of the devil, when it thinks of him at all, as some sort of comic figure with a pointy face, ears and mustache, wearing a red Edwardian tailcoat.

Every year modern viewers give evidence of Bosch's continued appeal by seeking out a special room in Vienna's Academy of Fine Arts, in which hangs an enormous triptych of the *Last Judgment*. It is far from being one of Bosch's best pictures. Fire has scorched one of the panels, and some of its surface has been rather badly retouched by later painters. In fact, art historians have been divided, particularly in recent years, about whether it is by Bosch himself or is the work of skilled copyists in his workshop. These debates need not concern us. For even if the painting is not pure Bosch, it provides a perfect introduction to the infernal landscape created by Bosch. Busy and complex as it at first seems, the picture is, for Bosch, relatively simple and straightforward. Its form is traditional: three panels present the *Fall of Man, the Last Judgment* and *Hell.* Above the *Last Judgment* a bland Christ Triumphant, come to judge the quick and the dead, sits on a small cloud. It is below Him that Bosch's astounding visions and strange symbols begin to take over the stage. From foreground to horizon the misshapen hosts of Satan outdo themselves in inflicting intricate violence on the vulnerable white flesh of innumerable Christian sinners.

In the near foreground something very like a duck-billed platypus, walking erect on a pair of human legs and carrying a bow, drags one of the damned home to some nether world cooking pot. Not far away a witch is simmering a child in a frying pan, and a toad in shining armor, mounted on the back of a naked woman, slashes away at the left arm of a male sinner tied to a tree. In one corner of this unhappy landscape a vast knife blade is being set into position to slice into a heap of writhing sinners. To the left a naked girl with a large praying mantis clinging to her legs is being ushered to bed by a dragon carrying a candle. Strange torture machines, ancestors to modern meat grinders, dot the scene. A pale pink dome, apparently constructed out of riveted metal segments, acts as a cover for batteries of guns firing on a cluster of victims helplessly impaled on a great thorn tree like mice made captive by some provident shrike. Farther off, the sulphurously glowing hell-fires cast circles of light on a murky, cratered landscape where yet more herds of naked sinners are being variously burned, poked and prodded. One unfortunate, saddled and bridled, is being briskly shod with red-hot horseshoes.

One of the many small shocks conveyed by such a picture is how modern it seems. Today we take the portrayal of cruelty and ugliness as the peculiar province of our own time, forgetting that earlier ages were encouraged to depict these horrors because, as one medieval churchman expressed it, "All that is deformed and repulsive awakes in us a longing for perfect beauty." The 20th Century, in fact, has been so preoccupied with sex, pain and perversion, as well as with the revelations of the subconscious, that it is possible in moments of exasperation to feel that such things were invented within the memory of living man, and then relentlessly popularized in the name of Freud.

Bosch's paintings are very much in vogue now. Within the last decade or so, a number of fat volumes devoted to his tortuous symbolism and titillating scenery have been written or reissued. A New York company specializing in expensive jigsaw puzzles cut to order from fine prints of old masters has even reported that Bosch's most mysterious and controversial painting, *The Garden of Delights (pages 60-63),* has become one of its most popular subjects. Bosch is also one of the few painters with the dubious honor of being written up not merely in art reviews but in medical journals, where psychiatrists muse learnedly about his sexual symbolism and speculate upon his possible insanity. Among other things, such critics have suggested that the fascination that this 15th Century painter exerts on 20th Century audiences derives from the fact that he isolated and portrayed man's archetypal fears—which include, as one distinguished psychoanalyst, in all seriousness, explained, our well-known "fear of being turned into trees."

But the modern fashion of viewing Bosch's paintings with owlish scientism and seeing the man himself as a semipsychotic mind explorer who first took the lid off the id 400 years before Freud, misses the main point. Judging from his pictures, Bosch was probably a man much inclined to rage against sinfulness and who took a pessimistic reading of human nature. But the outlandish doings in the Vienna *Last Judgment* and other pictures, far from being subconscious revelations, are intensely formal, highly self-conscious—if often fantastically complex—visualizations of signs and symbols, most of them familiar to people in Bosch's time.

What often looks to us like Freudian revelation is customarily a ploddingly literal picture of a Flemish proverb or a symbolic sin. In the *Last Judgment,* for instance, the girl with the praying mantis and the candle-holding dragon does not have an insect fetish. She is merely suffering the then well-known infernal punishment for lechery. A plump fellow being cruelly force fed is one kind of glutton. And the naked lady who appears in a number of Bosch paintings with a frog on her stomach was, at the time, a familiar symbol for the sin of pride.

The seven deadly sins, in fact, are relatively easy to decipher wherever they are depicted, because usually the punishment fits the crime. A sinner who snapped and snarled at his friends and family in life and so proved himself guilty of the sin of anger is likely to be found in hell being snapped at by packs of wild dogs—or stabbed by demons. He who indulged himself in overeating, as the art historian E. H. Gombrich once noted in summing up the difference between Bosch's time and our own, found his reward was not "an increase in cholesterol, but toads for breakfast in all eternity."

This kind of decoding is simple enough. But many of Bosch's paintings are harder to decipher because of his literal renderings of now-lost Flemish adages and his use of such things as fortunetelling tarot card devices, signs of the zodiac and alchemists' symbols. Here, attempts at freewheeling guesses would be disastrous. (Imagine what critics five centuries from now who had never heard of Mother Goose might do if asked to explain an illustration for Humpty Dumpty. That great egg might easily be interpreted as some sort of global fertility symbol, while poor Humpty's fall from the wall would wind up, no doubt, as symbolic of the fall in the Garden of Eden.)

The wide information gap caused by 500 years of change at first cuts the modern viewer off from much of Bosch's work and Bruegel's as well. Both artists were essentially engaged in a kind of program painting, which depended on their viewers' acquaintance with an incredible range of folklore and superstition, in just the way that a nightclub entertainer today counts on audience familiarity with such things as the Beatles' haircuts, Los Angeles' smog and General de Gaulle's long nose.

Wherever the information gap can be bridged—the exact proverb found, the exact riddle read—then Bosch and Bruegel paintings, which may have seemed like hallucinatory ramblings, become as clear as today's most pointed political cartoon. In the fabled realm of forgetful ease pictured in a Bruegel work called *Land of Cockaigne,* one vignette presents an egg sashaying around on human legs with a spoon stuck in its broken top and a pig rooting for acorns with a slice of ham cut from its back and the knife still invitingly stuck there. The scene at first seems not merely surrealistic, but a little sick. But then we discover a familiar legend that every Flemish and German child knew in Bruegel's time and most do today: if you eat your way through a mountain of gruel you come to a land where ham and eggs eagerly wait to run up and serve themselves to you, and geese fly already roasted into your mouth.

Proverbs, too, were a prime source of themes for Bosch and Bruegel—so much so that one of the best introductions to both painters is a long look at Bruegel's famous encyclopedic picture of over 100 Flemish proverbs *(pages 151-159)*—all, happily, identifiable. Many proverbs used by Bosch appear in Bruegel's painting, executed 40-odd years after Bosch's death, for folklore does not easily or swiftly change. But many other Boschian proverbs have yet to be found or have only recently come to light. For years one of the most puzzling enigmas in Bosch's work was the *Haywain.* Its central panel is dominated by an enormous soft-hued hay wagon with a pair of courtly lovers perched on top, while around them kings and peasants, priests and footpads grasp at the hay or belabor one another with inventive cruelty and cupidity. The *Haywain's* general meaning was clear enough, for the wagon is part of a triptych with the creation, temptation and fall of Adam and Eve at left and a hell panel at right, and it obviously is some sort of attack on the vanity of human wishes.

Reams of scholarly speculation were expended, however, before some astute detective work removed all doubt. Found in the writings of a Spanish scholar who lived just after Bosch's lifetime was an explanation that the word "hay" in Flemish meant "nothing." Thus the picture was a combined pun and riddle, deriding mankind's greedy search for the goods and pleasures of this world, all of which add up to *hooi*—meaning both "hay" and "nothing." As further evidence, it was recently discovered that in Antwerp in 1563 a giant hay wagon was dragged through the streets as part of a religious festival, while the accompanying crowd sang of how futile and fleeting is the pursuit of worldly goods.

A number of Bosch's intricate symbols have been interpreted *(see margin)*. Many have not. But even when their meaning is only partly grasped, Bosch's paintings bear witness to the fascinating fear of hell and the devil that tormented Europe for several centuries before, during and after the Reformation.

If the fear was of an intensity that we can no longer imagine, it is still possible, by considering the troubles of our own age, to understand the sense of precariousness and vulnerability that haunted so many of Bosch's contemporaries. Today, despite proof that science is more than ever capable of transforming our physical existence into something not far from a millennial heaven on earth, our faith in the moral perfectibility of man and society—which has served the modern world as something very like a religion for nearly a hundred years—has slowly dwindled. In its place have come doubts and fear of self-destruction. In the time of Bosch and Bruegel, too, faith was wavering; the physical fear of death was omnipresent. The medieval world had been orderly. For all its cruelty, life in feudal society had been protected from fear of physical death by an unshakeable faith that the body was merely a disposable sheath that briefly housed an immortal soul. By the mid-1400s, though, not only had the political order broken down, but men who saw that the Church was corrupt felt their spiritual bulwark had crumbled too. What if the devil proved to be God's match? What was to protect man from eternal death, from his own weakness and from Satan?

The 15th Century trembled before many troubling terrors and unsettling trends. Europe was swept by recurring bouts of the same plague that during the previous century had cut the population of the Continent in half. Artists turned out countless pictures of St. Sebastian—one of the saints to be prayed to for relief from the plague. In the climate of fear brought about by the Black Death, astrology, sorcery and dozens of heresies flourished as never before. Thousands of desperate folk joined processions of penitents who whipped each other with scourges in simple faith that the sinfulness of man alone brought such cruel judgment from heaven and that only by penance could they atone. It was the age, too, when gunpowder was first used in Europe; and a time when the public's idea of good fun was to lock a half dozen blind, starving and possibly mad citizens in a ring with big clubs and a small pig and watch them batter each other insensible trying to kill the pig in order to get a meal.

The era's broader historical events were hardly more reassuring. In 1453, near the time of Bosch's birth, Constantinople fell to the Turks. By storming this eastern bastion of Christendom the Turks opened the way for their successive assaults on Europe, which did not end until after Pieter Bruegel's death more than 100 years later. At about the same time, what we know now to have been the last battles of the Hundred Years' War involving France and England were fought. But at the time there was only uncertainty and, for many, the expectation that hostilities might break out again as they had so often done after periods of calm.

Death, in any case, became so appallingly present in the people's minds that it inspired a special kind of popular art. One example was a great

Bosch employed an incredible range of symbols in his paintings. Many have multiple meanings and seem to defy classification, for the artist drew upon a variety of sources. Weird animalistic images like those above are taken from Gothic manuscripts and may even go back as far as engraved Roman gems. A number of Bosch's symbols are used in traditional ways—the peacock and mirror usually signify pride; the rabbit indicates fertility. Still others seem traditional but take on unexpected meanings: the fish, for example, widely understood to stand for Christianity, was sometimes used by Bosch to suggest voraciousness. One of his most pervasive symbols, the bagpipe, shifts its meaning from painting to painting; it may represent gluttony or discord or have a significance that is lost today. Despite such confusions and complexities, Bosch used a number of relatively straightforward symbols whose meanings remain consistent. Some of these are listed below:

The Owl—heresy, evil
Fruit—sex, licentiousness
The Cat—cruelty, the devil
Stringed Instruments—love
The Horse—unbridled rage, lust
The Crescent—paganism, heresy
The Jug—gluttony
The Egg—life, the source of life
The Goat—prurience, lust

rash of woodcuts devoted to the Art of Dying. Sometimes their aim was to encourage Christians by showing how saints and martyrs, as well as the Blessed Virgin, serenely and piously met their deaths. Sometimes they showed an average man on the point of death being tempted by demons, and in this case, as with a picture like Bosch's *Death of a Miser,* their purpose might be to underline the folly of a misspent life. Another series, subject for woodcuts and paintings alike, showed the grim reaper laying low the great and small of the world. This theme reached its climax in art with Pieter Bruegel's *Triumph of Death* in which skeletal legions swarm like locusts over a whole landscape, doing in and dragging down to hell what seems to be the entire population of a small province.

The ostensible purpose for showing death at work was pious, to shock man into renouncing the seductive delights of this world by telling him, as the Bible had, that all flesh will be cut down like grass. But there also were egalitarian overtones in this art, for it emphasized that death took the rich as swiftly as the poor. And beyond this there must have been a large dose of simple superstition, the hopeful belief, which most of us secretly harbor, that by imagining the worst we can somehow avoid it.

Still, it is hard not to feel in such artistic fashions a sickening undercurrent of religious zeal gone wrong. Renunciation of the world founded on disgust and morbidity is not the teaching of Christian wisdom, as the Dutch historian Johan Huizinga observes in his renowned study of the period, *The Waning of the Middle Ages.* Yet this attitude seems to have darkened the spirit of the time. Nothing could be more chilling than Huizinga's description of the cemetery of the Church of the Innocents in Paris. "There," he writes, "the medieval soul, fond of a religious shudder, could take its fill of the horrible. . . . In order to make room it was necessary to dig up the bones and sell the tombstones after a very short time. It was believed that in this earth a human body was decomposed to the bone in nine days. Skulls and bones were heaped up in charnel-houses along the cloisters enclosing the ground . . . and lay there open to the eye by thousands. . . . Day after day crowds of people walked under the cloisters. . . . In spite of the incessant burials and exhumations going on, it was a public lounge and a rendezvous. Shops were established before the charnel-houses and prostitutes strolled under the cloisters."

By 1484, when Bosch was about 30 years old, Pope Innocent VIII in a portentous papal bull declared witchcraft to be a prime heresy of Christendom and set off a wave of fear and repression, of sadism and misogyny that resulted in the execution by burning and hanging of more than a hundred thousand women over the next two centuries. Witches, as everyone knew, had given themselves over to the devil for protection in this world, worshiping him in a dreadful, upside-down parody of the Mass and bringing propitiatory gifts to him in place of offerings to the Church. Five years after Innocent's bull, in 1489, two unsavory Dominican monks, Heinrich Krämer and Jakob Sprenger, produced a complete handbook for witch-hunters called *Malleus Maleficarum (The Witches' Hammer).* Profiting from the then recent development of the printing press, the book swiftly went to 30 editions and became one of Europe's earliest best sellers.

The modern reader is appalled by some of the enormities of this book —the outrageous finality with which it decrees that witches cannot weep, for instance, but that they can fly after rubbing their limbs with a special salve decocted from the limbs of human babies. To aid in establishing proof of witchcraft, the book explains that the devil always marks his witches in some nether part, either by an ice-cold kiss or the imprint of his clawlike left hand. Women suspected of witchcraft were therefore stripped and inspected—any kind of wart, blemish or birthmark being proof of guilt. In the fury of the moment, of course, charges were not always limited to women. Men and children were executed too. And in the stout Swiss city of Zurich, the citizenry, in 1497, even truly tried and hanged for sorcery a rooster accused of laying an egg.

Today we are astonished by the ignorance and fear that could have led the Catholic Church and then the newly formed Protestant sects to wage such a desperate war upon their helpless victims. Harder for us to understand is the desperation that led a number of women to actually take part in demonic rites, and there is much evidence that many of them did. Many women really believed that they were witches, in the sense that they forsook the Church and for protection had joined clandestine offshoots of an ancient pagan cult conducted by unscrupulous or deranged men and women. These groups held topsy-turvy versions of the Mass at which the leaders played the part of the devil in special black costumes and sometimes wore simulated horns and other phallic decorations to lend authenticity to their roles.

The goings on at such secret rites were seldom seen, but superstitious and educated people alike were quick to imagine the worst. Eventually a complete, savage litany for the witches' sabbath was formulated in the popular mind, a mixture of fact and fantasy, with the emphasis on fantasy. When Bosch was painting his *Temptation of St. Anthony (pages 64-65)* he did not have to retreat to any neurotic, private world to produce the parodied half-Mass, half-banquet taking place at a table by the outdoor altar rail where the troubled saint is kneeling. The blackamoor holding up a frog instead of the Host, the lively cripple, the piglike man in a black cassock wearing on his head an owl (a symbol of heresy) all were familiar communicants of the witches' sabbath. According to the modern Swiss theologian Walter Nigg the ritual included the use of toads in place of the Host, prayers that were recited backwards and dancing that grew "wilder and wilder until all were whirling madly, the cripples and lame dancing more lightly than those who were sound of limb." Afterwards, Nigg concludes, "the devil gave the witches lessons on how to transform themselves into cats and goats, how to cast the evil eye, how to raise hailstorms, how to make women barren and how to cause men to be impotent."

All these details may well have owed less to imagination than we now believe possible and more to the records of contemporary witch trials where, quite obviously, almost any supernatural charge was accepted as the literal truth. One trial record from the year 1565, when Bruegel was doing some of his greatest painting, matter-of-factly recounts that a Netherlandish girl named Digna Robert was taken in by the devil, posing as a "handsome young man dressed in a black cassock and calling himself Barrebon."

The tireless impresario who staged all these worldy torments commanded a cast of millions and went under many names besides Barrebon—Moloch, Beelzebub, Satan, the Prince of Darkness, to name but a few. To understand Bosch as the profoundly religious painter that he so clearly was, and to understand the age for which he painted, it is necessary not merely to believe in the possibility of the devil's existence but also to grasp the essential fact that the devil was a profoundly religious creation.

One of the Church's prime concerns was to justify God's way to man in a world that God had created but that found itself beset by plague, war and unspeakable cruelty. Because of this, if the devil had not existed, it would have been necessary to invent him. From the Scriptures he was, of course, already symbolically responsible for the evil in the world because, as the angel Lucifer, he had rebelled against God in Heaven and been thrown out by angelic hosts. In the Garden of Eden it was he, in the form of a serpent, who tempted Adam and Eve to their and all mankind's downfall.

Clearly, however, the more powerful and ubiquitous the devil seemed, and the more graphic his temptations and torments could be made, the more effective his image would be to scare corrupt mankind into virtuous behavior.

The revolution of the devil's religious role as a frightening villain in the war for men's souls began early. Certain ambiguous passages in the book of Revelation had prompted generations of Christians to predict a millennium, when the just would get their deserts, and the tired world would be reborn. For centuries the year 1000 was popularly considered to mark the inception of heaven on earth, and much medieval patience and piety was buttressed by hope for that great day. But by 1100 confidence that the millennium would come as predicted had faded. It was during this time that the devil's image began to be deformed from a beautiful, sulky angel into the grotesque and fearful figure, master of monsters and demons, that was to inflame the religious imagination of Europe for hundreds of years. Satan became a black prince of the world, the very symbol of eternal fear. His iniquitous brush touched everything earthly with the blacks of pitch, the hot reds and sickly sulphurs of the fiery furnace.

As Satan's stature grew, so too, in an opposite role, did that other great religious creation, the image of the Virgin Mary. Mary evolved from a remote, austere, theological symbol into the radiant Queen of Heaven, the gentle emblem of forgiveness and everlasting hope.

The flowering of Mary's image was reflected in religious art—which indeed was practically the only kind of art from the Ninth Century until sometime within the lifetime of Pieter Bruegel—and in church architecture as well. Sometimes serene, sometimes joyful, sometimes twisted in anguish as she mourns the dead Christ, the Virgin is the central figure of hundreds and hundreds of paintings—and often she is clothed in the dazzling colors of morning, white, gold and blue. The great Gothic cathedrals of northern Europe are mostly dedicated to

Holding a cloth filled with smiling figures representing souls, the enthroned prophet Abraham symbolically receives the saved in this cast of a detail from the portal sculpture of the Cathedral of St. Stephen in Bourges, France. St. Peter stands guard at the gate to the house—representing heaven—in which Abraham sits. Next to St. Peter is a monk, the first in line for salvation, while angels above hold crowns for heaven's newcomers. Treatment of the damned, another portion of the same sculpture, is shown opposite.

her, and she was the glowing subject of their stained-glass windows and their statuary alike.

The devil appears far less often. He tends to be represented by the hosts of demons who did his bidding. The evolution of his image, too, may be traced in art, where it is most clearly observable in subjects like the Last Judgment and the Temptations of St. Anthony, which Flemish painters made peculiarly their own.

One of the best of the early *Last Judgments,* done long before oil painting on panels was invented, is a stone relief on the west portal of the 13th Century cathedral in the French city of Bourges. Everything is quite orderly. Christ sits on an upper level. The scene below him is divided exactly in half by the tall figure of the archangel Michael holding the scales that weigh men's souls. Scrupulously, the damned and the saved are given equal space to right and left. Looking at the doorway as a whole, however, it is easy to see why the Frenchman who has the postcard concession in Bourges today does not sell many cards showing the saved: they stand at left in attitudes of static piety, like so many bland statues. What the eyes of Bourges citizens passing through the portal are drawn toward is the scene on the right, where the naked and the damned are being herded toward a hell mouth that looks like the head of an enormous and thoroughly angry tom cat lying flat on the floor upside down. Flames flicker out of his mouth where attendant devils have placed a pot loaded with the first pair of sinners.

Yet it is impossible to imagine these proceedings ever getting out of hand. For one thing, Christ Triumphant is firmly fixed above it all. For another, the archangel Michael, who after all had been largely responsible for throwing Lucifer out of heaven in the first place, looks strong-shouldered and brawnily wholesome, while the devils are nubbly little folk, a kind of subrace of spavined janitors.

The same sense of divine control is imposed on artistic representations of the devil and his doings for the next 200 years. Even Van Eyck's *Last Judgment* painted in 1420-1425, although it includes demons embodied as serpents and assorted deep-sea monsters, conveys the feeling that Michael and Christ have the devil and his minions bottled up in hell.

To go from that scene to any of Bosch's various hells, however, is like opening the door of a blast furnace. Both literally and figuratively Bosch lets loose hell-fire for the first time. It burns not merely in hell but across the surface of the world. The archangel Michael has disappeared. Christ Triumphant has shrunk to a tiny figure floating in a narrow strip of sky. The border between man and beast, between the devil's world and God's has been breached, and there is no telling where, on earth, one ends and the other begins. Only the Garden of Eden, the scene of Satan's first victory over man, remains unchanged. The results are either the most effective artistic preachments against sin in history, or an unintentional heresy, the blazing apotheosis of the devil.

Whatever his didactic achievement, Bosch succeeds as a painter of diabolic scenes not because he is so relentless in showing the practice and punishment of sin but because somehow, almost magically, he makes the devil's torments hot to the touch. Earlier versions of similar scenes seem

Demons herd the damned toward the fiery caldron of hell in this detail of the sculpture over the main doors of the Cathedral of St. Stephen. The sinners, including a crowned king and two mitred bishops, are shown preparing for their first scalding taste of the eternal torments that await them. The pot bubbles in the blazing breath of a monster representing hell itself, while toads, other devilish weapons of punishment, bite the tongue of a scandalmonger and the breast of a lecherous woman.

academic to a modern viewer; their stylized sinners are removed from life, their demons seem like comic strip villains who shoot without drawing blood or poke with fiery pitchforks but do not burn their victims. And after Bosch, the devil's henchmen soon take on a theatrical self-consciousness, like the stagy monsters in Grünewald's *Temptation of St. Anthony* who should be terrifying but today look as if they are costumed for a play.

The differences in various painters' treatment of hell's torments and the devil, of course, may owe more to artistic convention than to the religious feelings of the individual painter. When it came to painting his *Last Judgment,* Michelangelo naturally presented monumental human forms in motion rather than bestial creatures. This is not to say that Michelangelo felt the power of hell less fiercely than Bosch did. But looking at Michelangelo's painting, it is hard not to feel that he looked on the *Last Judgment* mainly as an occasion for painting a splendid picture, while Bosch's visions seem to reek of hell itself.

For the Church or a painter to preach fear of the devil by reveling in the torments of the damned put both of them on a precarious ecclesiastical tightrope. The artist was faced with an exquisite problem: was he painting these horrors because he hated them or because he sinfully enjoyed them? As the delicate brush tips the demon's wing with an angelic touch of white, as the master's hand traces the soft curve of a naked sinner's glowing cheek, how easy for the secret heart to stir guiltily and the man to find himself suddenly a victim of the devil's wiles. Such men in Bosch's time must have felt themselves constantly in danger, as doctors and nurses today do who work in plague areas and run the risk of being killed by the very diseases they come to cure.

Was Bosch infected? No one knows. Some scholars, intrigued by the strangeness of some of his symbols as well as by the breathtaking beauty of some of his scenes depicting sin, have suspected that Bosch belonged to some secret heretical sect. The few known facts about Bosch's life lend little support to such theories. The painter appears to have been much respected in 's Hertogenbosch, where he piously played Christmas music for his church and was a member of the influential and orthodox Brotherhood of the Holy Virgin. Moreover, he is known to have painted at least one altarpiece, now lost, for the local Cathedral of St. John.

In the absence of biographical evidence, the search has centered on the paintings themselves, especially upon the real meaning of Bosch's strange masterpiece, *The Garden of Delights (pages 60-63).* The picture can be taken as an orthodox presentation of sinfulness and torment. But in recent years it has been read in many ways, some based upon Freudian psychology, others stemming from long study of 15th Century sects and symbols. The most ingenious and detailed theory so far is one which insists plausibly that the painting actually illustrates the rituals of the Adamites, a heretical nudist sect with many followers in Brabant, whose central notion was that man should prepare for God's reign on earth by discarding his lust and sense of sin and worshiping together without clothes in the innocence of Adam and Eve. No theory advanced to date is conclusive, however, and whether or not Bosch was of the devil's party without being aware of his error remains a mystery.

For the Church the problem of preaching about the devil was crucial. If Satan seemed too real and fear of him grew too great, quaking Christians were likely to fall into the heresy of believing that the devil was God's equal and the world his private province. Many people did just that, and their fear lay at the heart of what was, from the Church's point of view, the greatest and most successful heresy of all time—the Protestant Reformation. The devil, Martin Luther observed (and he wrote of having encountered the devil personally on a number of occasions), was too strong, the world too worldly and man too weak to resist temptation through his own efforts or to be saved through the intercession of the organized Church. Mixing total pessimism with miraculous optimism Luther decided that man could be saved from the devil only by the pure, inscrutable and undeserved mystery of God's grace.

It was in 1517 that Luther nailed his famous theses to the church door in Wittenberg. Hieronymus Bosch had died the year before, and Pieter Bruegel was born less than a decade later. When he began painting, the Reformation was reaching full strength. Art historians have pointed out that in painting like Bosch, Bruegel was indulging in self-conscious archaism, and stylistically this is true. But emotionally, Bruegel was working close to the frontier of popular Flemish feeling. To Bruegel's audience the devil was still very much abroad, hell-fires were still blazing, and Bosch's demons were still nailing red-hot horseshoes to the feet of sorry sinners.

Demons and hearty workmen share a perch astride flying buttresses on the Cathedral of St. John in 's Hertogenbosch, Flanders, where Hieronymus Bosch was born. The architects of the building, which was worked on from the end of the 14th Century until well into the 16th Century, saw nothing incongruous in this juxtaposition; they also placed a stonemason close to a scowling man-beast reading a book. Bosch's painted imagery may well owe a debt to the tradition of combining the fantasic with the real.

Bosch: Dark Dreams and Demons

The bizarre image opposite is the creation of the world's most provocative and enigmatic artist—Hieronymus Bosch. He died in the Brabant town of 's Hertogenbosch in 1516, barely a decade before the birth of Bruegel. Like the Flemish masters who preceded him, Bosch was a passionately religious artist. But his paintings, unlike theirs, revealed the dark strain of fear and pessimism that often underlay the serene piety of the age. In pictures unmatched in art, Bosch unleashed the scalding fires of hell upon earth and sent demonic monsters to torment long-suffering saints and naked sinners. Bosch's message—that fire and brimstone await every man—was clear. But in delivering it the painter used tangles of symbols from remote sources—including the writings of Flemish mystics and the lore of the alchemists. So absorbing are these hieroglyphics that they distract attention from Bosch's brilliant use of color and landscape. Modern attempts to decipher the symbolism, moreover, have stirred great controversy. Focusing most sharply on one remarkable picture, *The Garden of Delights,* the argument has raised questions ranging from whether Bosch was a secret, heretical admirer of the devil, to the possibility that his art is merely the outpouring of a troubled unconscious. Predictably, no sure answers can be found. But such questions serve as a fascinating introduction into the complex world of a painter who is as easy to enjoy as he is hard to understand.

This improbable creature looming out of a tranquil setting is a familiar Boschian symbol. It combines an egg and a tree—both representing the original source of life—with carousing drinkers (inside the egg) to warn that man and all earthly creations are innately corrupt. An owl and a half-moon flag (to symbolize heresy) reinforce Bosch's indictment of the world. The Bruegel signature was perhaps added by a collector in order to enhance the drawing's value.

Hieronymus Bosch: *The Human Tree,* date unknown

Hieronymus Bosch: *Cripples and Beggars*, date unknown

The striking similarity between Bosch's sketches of cripples and beggars and those later painted by Bruegel points up Bosch's influence on the younger artist. The crammed page also emphasizes a neglected aspect of Bosch's genius—the sound drawing and sharp eye for realism that lend authority to his wildest fancies and macabre caricatures. Even in a relatively simple painting like the *Ship of Fools (opposite)*, realistic detail is blended with didactic symbolism. A popular metaphor for the

fecklessness of human society, the ship, in Bosch's handling, is crewed by personifications of the deadly sins— Gluttony, for example, is getting soused in the rigging, and Anger is about to bash her shipmate with a jug. Outrage at corrupt ecclesiastics was so widespread in Bosch's time that the painter did not hesitate to present Lust in the forms of a monk and a nun enjoying a plate of cherries and playing music (two symbols of unchastity), while they gamely try to catch a swinging pastry ball in their teeth.

Hieronymus Bosch: *Ship of Fools*, 1475-1480

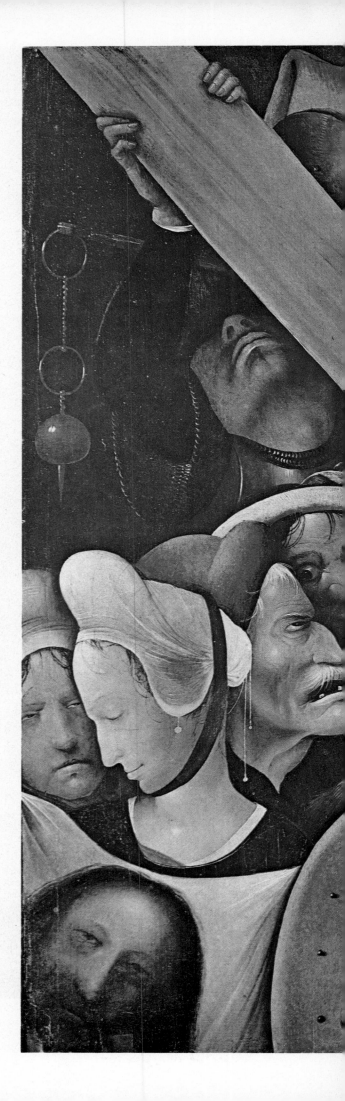

Bosch's pictures of sinners being set upon by the demons of hell are terrifying. But, as his *Carrying of the Cross* shows, it is in the unflinching exposure of the bestiality of man toward man that the painter can often be most shocking. Better than any other artist Bosch captured the insane lust for violence characteristic of a vindictive mob in his day or our own, or on the hill of Golgotha outside Jerusalem some 2,000 years ago. The grotesques pressing around Christ are extremes of caricature. Yet their pop–eyed, jeering rage and their frenzied anticipation of the cruelty to come are recognizably human.

A traditional subject for religious art, *The Carrying of the Cross* customarily included a much larger view of the proceedings. Bosch heightened the impact of his picture by stripping away all the surrounding action, leaving only a handful of hateful faces, seen large and seeming to float on a black background. At their center is the suffering Christ with eyes serenely closed, apparently oblivious to the nightmare around Him. The only other peaceful expression in the crowd belongs to St. Veronica, who has just wiped the sweat from Jesus' face and has been rewarded for this act of charity by the imprint of His image on her veil. To intensify his savage satire Bosch included the two thieves who shared Christ's fate and who are normally portrayed on crosses beside Him. The repentant thief *(upper, right)* is being rewarded for his last-minute return to piety by the harangue of a half-demented, snaggle-toothed monk and the glowering stare of a pompous magistrate. The other thief *(bottom, right),* unrepentant to the end, glares clench-jawed at three buffoons who mock him. Ugly as he is, Bosch has made him less repulsive than his righteous tormentors.

Hieronymus Bosch: *The Carrying of the Cross*, c. 1505

Hieronymus Bosch: *The Garden of Delights*, c.1500

In some ways *The Garden of Delights,* Bosch's most mysterious picture, is starkly simple. It presents life as a morality play in three acts. The show opens with God creating Eve in the Garden *(left panel),* moves to the sinful high noon of worldly life *(center panel)* and closes amidst the torments of hell. In Bosch's time zealous Christians looked upon even the beauties of the world as the snare of the devil. For them, foolish Eve and all women thereafter were prime instruments of man's temptation. Not surprisingly they took the forbidden fruit—apples and, by extension, strawberries, cherries and plums, too—as symbols for sweet licentiousness. Seen in these harsh, symbolic terms Bosch's central panel is simply an orgy. In the foreground lustful swimmers tear at a large floating blackberry, and elsewhere couples embrace inside giant strawberries. One amorous reclining sinner is baldly provided with a plum for a head. In the upper center *(detail below)* a group of naked girls cavort in the pond. Around them ride men mounted on animals that represent bestial vitality and fecundity. Most pictorial attacks on human depravity, including earlier efforts by Bosch himself, tended to make physical sin ugly. But Bosch's sinners, dwarfed by large birds and fruits so that they look like tiny fairytale creatures, seem graceful and innocent-looking no matter what they are doing. Strange inconsistencies and enigmatic combinations of symbols (like the mouse in the glass tube) all combine to suggest that Bosch was also dealing with intricate, interlocked levels of meaning that far exceed straightforward preachment. For decades critics have searched for a key to unlock these meanings. Those students with a Freudian background, for example, noting the abundance of clinically catalogued sexuality, assert that Bosch was merely giving free play to his lustful unconscious. A parallel theory suggests that Bosch painted the picture to illustrate the doctrine of an heretical sect known as the Adamites, whose members sought a return to the innocence of Eden by shedding both their clothes and the ingrained medieval belief that the human body is ugly and sinful. Such theories are inconclusive. The beauty of Bosch's sinners probably had a simpler explanation. As a sophisticated moralist, Bosch knew the devil to be an ultra-sophisticated tempter. In his picture the painter was doing explicit justice to the seductive delights that lead men to damnation.

These two details from *The Garden of Delights* show the great range of Bosch's invention—from the pastoral serenity of Eden *(above)* to the nightmares of hell. There, *(clockwise from the lower left)*, drinkers and gamblers are assailed by avenging monsters; musical instruments become the tools of torture for sinners who have corrupted the harmony of the world; men who have eaten too well are swallowed by a devil bird who voids them into the nether world; a pig dressed as an abbess reveals ecclesiastical avarice by trying to have a doomed man sign his wealth

over to the Church. Punishments seem to fit the crime, but certain objects, like the sled at the upper right, are undeciphered. Even Bosch's handling of the Garden is equivocal. Some animals, like the rabbits, are normal, some, like those around the pool, are hybrid creatures.

Church doctrine held that neither sin nor death existed on earth before man brought them into being by eating the forbidden fruit. But Bosch shows a proud cat with its kill. No one knows whether this is simply a naturalistic detail or a hint that paradise was corrupt before the fall of man.

Hieronymus Bosch: *The Temptation of St. Anthony*, c.1500

A few lines from a popular account of the life of St. Anthony describe how the holy man was set upon by fiends in the shape of horrid beasts, beautiful ladies and "hideous giants" who tried to distract him from his meditations. Bosch's age turned these few lines into a fantastic subject for religious art. None of the *Temptations of St. Anthony* are richer or wilder than Bosch's version shown here. In what is known as "continuous narrative," the saint appears four times. He can be seen twice in the left-hand panel: first praying while being flown about on the back of an aerial monster *(top),* then, after fainting and falling to earth, being dragged along by helpful friends *(below)* whose melancholy leader may be a self-portrait of Bosch. In the center panel, kneeling outside a crumbling ruin, Anthony tries to keep his mind on the figure of Christ in the alcove, despite a Black Mass being conducted by a long-snouted, beastly, bespectacled bishop, and the celebration of a witches' sabbath taking place beside him at the altar. Seated in the right panel, the saint studies the Scriptures to keep his mind off a naked girl and the mysterious table in the foreground. Some of Bosch's demons and symbols are perversions of Christian practice like the upside-down church service at the witches' sabbath, where the elevated Host is a frog holding an egg. Others are the precise opposite of Christian symbols. The bird in the left-hand panel shown eating its young in the shell is entirely unlike the pelican, a symbol of Christ's sacrifice because it cared for its young so well. Bosch's depiction of hell-fire helped to inspire *Mad Meg (next pages),* one of several paintings by Pieter Bruegel that could be taken for Bosch's own work. In presenting what seems to be a fragment of a folk tale about an angry giantess who led an army of Flemish housewives in a war on hell, Bruegel made good use of many Boschian creatures, from rotten eggs and stumpy monsters to voracious fish with legs.

Pieter Bruegel: *Dulle Griet (Mad Meg)*, 1562

III

"Peasant" Bruegel

A handsome yet strangely melancholy portrait of two monkeys chained in a massive tower also shows, in the distance, the waterfront section of Antwerp where Bruegel lived in 1562 when he painted the picture. Monkeys were commonly used to represent man's bondage to his bestial side, and the picture can be seen as a blend of local scenery and didactic commentary on human weakness. In the 1560s, moreover, Bruegel's resentful countrymen felt that they were held in chains by the Spanish authorities in the Low Countries, which has led to the suspicion that the painting perhaps had a political meaning too.

Two Monkeys, 1562

Sitting back on the sidewalk seats of the Pieter Brueghel Café (H.J.J. Kuipers, Prop.) in the Brabant village of Brueghel a traveler today may sip a draft of the local beer and take in a most Bruegelian scene. The town is hardly an hour from both Amsterdam and Antwerp, but its single street is likely to carry far fewer cars than cart horses. An occasional white-coifed nun sputters shakily by on her motor bike. Through the spaces between the squat houses that line the road opposite the cafés, the visitor catches a glimpse of tall poplars fluttering beside small fields; dank clumps of grasses that tuft the banks of a tiny, cozy stream; tumbled-down thatched cottages with blunted gables dozing behind lines of ruthlessly trimmed willow stumps.

It is temptingly easy to imagine the young Pieter Bruegel (his name still spelled with an "h") growing up here. After all Bruegel *was* known for centuries as "Peasant" Bruegel. In his time, certainly, countryfolk migrating to a big city like Antwerp (as he did) customarily adopted the name of their home village. Besides, just down the road from the café, confidently confirming this line of thought, a stone obelisk proclaims the town's pride in its one illustrious son, Pieter Brueghel the Elder.

The fact is, though, that no one really knows where (or even when) the painter was born. Anyone trying to pinpoint these and many other basic biographical details of Pieter Bruegel's life is constantly frustrated by conflicting evidence or stymied by a complete lack of it. There is, for example, another town, also called Brueghel, also claiming to be the painter's birthplace, with as much, or as little, reason. Similarly, in establishing exactly when the painter was born, it is necessary to proceed by hints and guesses. The presently accepted date, 1525, was arrived at by working backward from a known date, 1551, the year of Bruegel's admission to the Antwerp painters' guild, and then assuming that Bruegel, like many of his colleagues, became a master painter at about age 26.

The authentic contemporary references to Bruegel's life are few—hardly more than a half dozen documents still exist. Among them: the listing that records his acceptance in the painters' guild as master in 1551; two letters written in 1561 and 1565 by the Italian geographer Scipio Fabius in Bologna to the famous Antwerp cartographer Abraham Ortelius inquiring after the health of their mutual friend "Petrus Bruochl"—whom Fabius remembered warmly from an encounter during the painter's trip to Italy in the 1550s; a notation in a Brussels church register in the summer of 1563 showing that Bruegel on that day married Mayken, daughter of Pieter Coeck van Aelst, painter, and Mayken Verhulst, herself a well-known watercolorist and painter of miniatures. No burial record exists, but there is good evidence that he died September 5, 1569. He was buried in Notre Dame de la Chapelle in Brussels. We know, too, that when Bruegel's young wife died, nine years later, it was the painter's mother-in-law, Mayken Verhulst, who cared for and began the artistic training of his two sons, Pieter Brueghel the Younger, born in 1564, and Jan Brueghel, born in 1568, less than a year before his father's death.

Happily, besides this handful of hard facts, there exists an intriguing 1,200-word account of Bruegel's life, published 35 years after his death. It appeared in 1604 in a volume entitled *Het Schilder-Boeck* (The Book of Painters) by Carel van Mander, dean of the Haarlem painters' guild. This convivial Dutchman tried to do for some three dozen Flemish and Dutch artists what his literary model, Italian art chronicler Giorgio Vasari, had done half a century earlier for the masters of the Renaissance in his admiring *Lives of the Painters*.

Van Mander proved a diverting chronicler and a character in his own right—as indeed any painter remembered mainly for his writing would have to be. The *Schilder-Boeck* is an often significant, frequently fanciful, sometimes inaccurate pousse-café of a book, which mingles classical learning and chatty anecdote, assembled with a journalist's weakness for a snappy phrase. Throughout, in Van Mander's evaluation of painters, a fashionable fondness for all things Italian struggles with a stubborn Dutch loyalty to the Northern tradition. Ignoring some painters entirely, Van Mander slights others and mixes up the names of still others because, as he remarks with disarming frankness, "I am not really up on those painters." The relatives and pupils of famous artists whom he interviewed to collect background material on subjects both living and dead frequently offered material, he grumbles, "more fit to fill a kitchen cupboard" than a book conceived for the greater glory of Art generally and Dutch and Flemish art in particular.

The *Schilder-Boeck*'s chapter devoted to Pieter Bruegel is vintage Van Mander, justly famous as a remarkably readable account. "In a wonderful manner," it begins with breathless enthusiasm, "Nature found and laid hold of the man who in his turn was destined to lay hold of Nature so magnificently, when in an obscure village in Brabant she chose from among the peasants, as the delineator of peasants, the witty and gifted Pieter Bruegel, and made of him a painter to the lasting glory of our Netherlands."

Van Mander then gets down to specifics. "He was born not far from Breda in a village named Brueghel, a name he took for himself and handed on to his descendants. He learned his craft from Pieter Coeck van Aelst, whose daughter he later married. When he lived with Van Aelst, she was a little girl whom he often carried about in his arms. On leaving

Van Aelst he went to work with Hieronymus Cock, and then he traveled to France and then to Italy. He did much work in the manner of Hieronymus Bosch and produced many spookish scenes and drolleries, and for this reason many called him Pieter the Droll. There are few works by his hand that the observer can contemplate solemnly and with a straight face. . . . On his journeys Bruegel did many views from nature so that it was said of him, when he traveled through the Alps, that he had swallowed all the mountains and rocks and spat them out again, after his return, onto his canvases and panels. . . . He settled down in Antwerp and there entered the painters' guild in the year of our Lord 1551. He did a great deal of work for a merchant, Hans Franckert, a noble and upright man, who found pleasure in Bruegel's company and met him every day. With this Franckert, Bruegel often went out into the country to see the peasants at their fairs and weddings. Disguised as peasants they brought gifts like the other guests, claiming relationship or kinship with the bride or groom. Here Bruegel delighted in observing the droll behavior of the peasants, how they ate, danced, drank, capered or made love."

The account goes on with some intriguing personal details. "As long as he lived in Antwerp, he kept house with a servant girl. He would have married her but for the fact that, having a marked distaste for the truth, she was in the habit of lying, a thing he greatly disliked. He made an agreement or contract with her to the effect that he would procure a stick and cut a notch in it for every lie she told, for which purpose he deliberately chose a fairly long one. Should the stick become covered with notches in the course of time, the marriage would be off, and there would be no further question of it. And indeed, this came to pass after a short time. In the end, when the widow of Pieter Coeck was living in Brussels, he courted her daughter whom, as we have said, he had often carried about in his arms, and married her. The mother, however, demanded that Bruegel should leave Antwerp and take up residence in Brussels, so as to give up and put away all thoughts of his former girl. And this indeed he did. He was a very quiet and thoughtful man, not fond of talking but ready with jokes when in the company of others. He liked to frighten people, often even his own pupils, with all kinds of spooks and uncanny noises. . . . We would be hard put to it to enumerate all the things he has painted, the weird and fantastic pictures, the pictures of hell and of peasants . . . with many comic figures, showing the true character of the peasants. . . . Many of his compositions of comical subjects, strange and full of meaning, can be seen engraved; but he made many more works of this kind in careful and beautifully finished drawings to which he added inscriptions. But as some of them were too biting and sharp, he had them burned by his wife when he was on his deathbed, from remorse or for fear that she might get into trouble and might have to answer for them."

Only two small engraved portraits that are thought to be of Bruegel exist today. Both show the painter with a massive head, an enormous nose and a patriarchal beard. It is most attractive to think of this august personage as Van Mander portrays him in words—a raw-wristed young apprentice lugging his master's baby daughter among the paint pots, or

PETRO BRVEGEL, PICTORI.

The stocky, bearded figure in this engraving may be an accurate likeness of Pieter Bruegel. The print was made by Bruegel's contemporary, Philipp Galle, and bears a Latin verse at the bottom that declares Bruegel to be the imaginative and witty successor of the old master Bosch.

later, cutting that big stick and gravely notching it each time his mistress told him a pretty white lie. Not surprisingly, anecdotes such as these have clung to Bruegel's image through the centuries.

Most of them, though entirely unverifiable, are probably true enough. Yet Van Mander's account is the source of at least one enduring misconception—the legend that Bruegel was merely a talented, oafish peasant. It was perfectly natural for Van Mander to emphasize the peasant side of "Pieter the Droll." Bruegel's peasant pictures were the precursors of the secular and saucy pictorial anecdotes so popular among Dutch painters and buyers a generation later in Van Mander's time. A broader consideration, however, made on the basis of the great intellectual range of his painting subjects, the quality of his friends and patrons (including the cartographer Ortelius) suggests that Bruegel was not a gifted bumpkin but a most worldly and cultivated man.

As to Bruegel's political and religious views, it is understandable that Van Mander, a Dutch nationalist and a Protestant in the newly independent land of Holland, should have assumed that Bruegel was a not-so-covert sympathizer with the Protestant rebels. But the artist's existing drawings and paintings, although they bear dramatic witness to much of the history of the times, are clearly the work of someone who, either from inclination or prudence, was at pains to avoid showing partisanship.

What Van Mander proved most right about was the importance of the painter's Italian journey. For Bruegel, then working for printmaker Hieronymus Cock, did make the fashionable pilgrimage south to see the great works of the High Renaissance. Had he run true to his times, as did the Flemish court painters Bernard van Orley and Frans Floris, he would have acquired an Italian patron and trudged home with a head stuffed with modish Romanist fancies for monumental nude figures, Greek columns and scenes from classical antiquity—all suitable for framing. Instead, he brought back a lifetime supply of landscape details, which he used with telling effect in many of his works. They also have provided history with a few visual clues as to where and how he traveled.

Bruegel was probably sent south by Hieronymus Cock to collect material for one of Cock's new series of engravings, either in the fall of 1551 or early spring of the next year. No one would have tried the Alps in midwinter. Bruegel's natural path lay south along the Meuse River into the Burgundy country, down the Saône as far as Lyons (where he sketched a view of the city), then northeast up the Rhône into Geneva. That uneasy city was in the process of being galvanized into a Protestant dictatorship by John Calvin, the Protestant theologian whose incendiary religious writings had recently been outlawed throughout the Low Countries by Charles V.

By 1552 Bruegel was over the Alps and far south in Italy, in Calabria on the Straits of Messina between Italy and Sicily. A signed pen-and-ink drawing shows the mainland seaport of Reggio burning, and history obligingly records that the city was put to the torch by Suleiman's Turkish sea raiders in 1552. In that same view of Reggio there appears a ragged, saw-toothed range of mountains that also turns up in Bruegel's engraving called *The Sea Battle in the Straits of Messina*. That scene shows a detailed view of the Italian coast observed from the Sicilian side, where the artist must also have traveled.

It is hard to know whether the Sicilian side trip occurred before or after Bruegel's visit to Rome. At some point, probably after Rome, he visited Naples at least long enough to make precise sketches for a future painting, *The Harbor of Naples*. Finished in 1563, it is one of the earliest seascapes with ships ever done in oils, and it is the only surviving painting by Bruegel of a precise locality. Leaving Naples, Bruegel made a slow progress northward toward Flanders, lingering long in the Alps, swinging east into Austria, probably as far as Innsbruck, and then doubling back to sketch a valley at Waltensburg in Switzerland.

However great his preoccupation with landscape, one overriding professional purpose of Bruegel's trip was a long stay in Rome. In this he was following in the footsteps of Northern artists who had first been attracted to the city during the brief papacy of a Netherlander, Adrian VI, a quarter of a century earlier. After Bruegel's time, in the 17th Century, when Rome blossomed into the center of the art world, Flemish painters would flock there in even greater numbers. But in the mid-16th Century, when Bruegel reached Rome, the city was still recovering from a disaster. Hardly a generation before, in 1527, it had been sacked twice within six months by the hired armies of Charles V. Charles, who wanted to cow the Pope into submission to Spain, had intended the troops more as a threat than an invasion force. But the soldiers were left unpaid, and their commander averted mutiny only by giving his men a free hand in looting Rome. When the news reached him in far-off Madrid, Charles was so mortified that he canceled all the festivities planned to celebrate the recent birth of his son and heir, the boy who would become Philip II. At least equally perturbed, Italian artists fled Rome to seek protection from other patrons—most notably Francis I. The ambitious French monarch, busy building châteaux on the Loire and beautifying his palace at Fontainebleau, eagerly bought up Italian Renaissance artists by the square yard.

Nevertheless, Rome, when Bruegel arrived, was still full of inspiration for a painter. Artistically it was the city of the aging Michelangelo. The Sistine Chapel ceiling provided generations of painters with an inexhaustible supply of Renaissance figures and poses. In later works—the *Last Judgment* done on the altar wall of the Sistine Chapel and the frescoes in Pope Paul III's private chapel—Michelangelo's art had taken on a different character. Though the figures in the two frescoes, the *Conversion of St. Paul* and the *Crucifixion of St. Peter*, retained their classical grandeur, they represented a turning away from High Renaissance ideals of harmony and balance in art. What Michelangelo was turning toward was Mannerism, a 16th Century movement in art that is most difficult to pin down but that is often characterized by elongated figures, unnatural body positions and odd color mixtures. Eventually, too, Mannerism came to encompass the custom of putting the main subject of a painting somewhere off-center, or even in the background, while thematically irrelevant details loomed mastodon-tall in the foreground. This practice Pieter Bruegel was to adapt for several paintings of Biblical subjects,

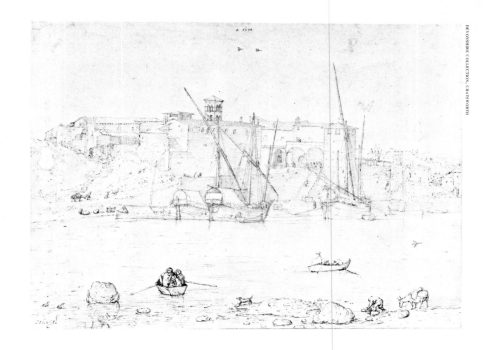

Among the few presumed souvenirs of Bruegel's stay in Italy is this pen-and-ink drawing of the Ripa Grande, Rome's port on the Tiber River. Drawings of the same scene by other artists confirm that the sketch was made on the spot, but the fact that the cloister and church tower in the background are drawn in a lighter ink seems to indicate that the darker foreground was added later. Some scholars believe that the addition, or perhaps even the entire sketch, was drawn not by Bruegel himself but by his artist son Jan, who also spent time in Italy.

including, as we have seen, *The Carrying of the Cross (pages 108-111).*

Little actual evidence is left to prove it, but Bruegel clearly must have made good use of his sketchbook in Rome. A figure of a man digging, taken from the Noah panel of the Sistine ceiling, turns up years later in Bruegel's black and white drawing of a Renaissance garden created for one of Hieronymus Cock's print series on the four seasons. Absorbing architecture as well as art, Bruegel apparently made sketches of the ruins of the Colosseum—at least it clearly served him as a model for one of his favorite subjects, the *Tower of Babel.* And there is an actual sketch of a riverside scene at Ripa Grande on the Tiber not far from Rome.

In addition to his drawing, Bruegel also seems to have kept busy as a painter. The records show that while in Rome he made friends with the Italian miniaturist Giulio Clovio and was asked to collaborate with him on several pictures. Clovio, an adopted Roman who migrated from Yugoslavia, is now largely forgotten. But in his own time Clovio was well known. Vasari, for instance, praises him as *un piccolo e nuovo* Michelangelo (loose translation: "a new mini-Michelangelo"). Among the possessions listed in Clovio's will is a painting for which, in the collaborative custom of the time, he supplied the human figures while Bruegel filled in the landscape background. Clovio's estate papers also refer to two other paintings "by the hand of Master Pieter Bruegel" *(di mano di M^{ro} Pietro Brugole),* probably given to Clovio by the painter along with the view of Lyons already mentioned. The two works, both now lost, were a small *Tower of Babel* on ivory and a watercolor of a tree.

One thing is certain. By the time he returned home in 1554, Bruegel had accumulated scores of landscape drawings and was ready, as Van Mander suggests, to spit out the Alps in various artistic ways. Like nearly all of Bruegel's later drawings these early landscapes were first roughed out in charcoal, in the field, and later made more precise with ink details. Like his many subsequent drawings, most of these scenes still exist, either in the original or as part of the many series of popular prints sold to the public by Hieronymus Cock.

Prints made from designs carved in wood blocks were first made around 1400, half a century before the invention of the first printing presses. Engravings—prints from lines incised in copper plates—soon followed. But it was not until the 16th Century that the proliferation of presses and improvements in printing techniques combined to make printmaking for a popular market a potentially big business. Hieronymus Cock, a minor landscape expert who journeyed to Italy in the 1530s, was among the first in the Netherlands to take advantage of the commercial opportunities in printmaking. He set up a business in his Antwerp house, which he called the House of the Four Winds.

The Four Winds Printshop, as a combined art dealing center, coffee-house and informal hangout for intellectuals, became a Netherlands landmark. From it, for 20 years starting in 1548, Cock dominated the print trade in the Low Countries. At first he catered mainly to the existing fashion for prints that were small black and white copies of famous paintings. But soon he was branching out—offering original engravings of local landscape scenes and such subjects as various versions of *The Seven Deadly Sins* and illustrations of proverbs, as well as original views of Flemish folk activities such as fairs, fights and drinking bouts.

The process of copying an oil painting in an engraving required an intermediate step: translation of the original work into a simple sharp-lined sketch. This sketch was then copied by an artisan who engraved the plate from which the print was made. To make the "translations," Cock gathered a coterie of gifted young artists who often worked anonymously. This was how Pieter Bruegel probably got his commercial start just before the trip to Rome. He seems to have learned much by copying—especially from Hieronymus Bosch, scores of whose works were sold by Cock in print form. Bruegel's energy and genius soon earned him a reputation and the right to draw and paint original works, using Boschlike subjects in a Boschlike style. Such original drawings were at first translated by Cock into engravings and sold as the work of Bosch. Bruegel's picture *Big Fish, Little Fish,* for example—a signed drawing illustrating the cannibalistic aspect of nature—turned up in one of Cock's early print series with *Hieronymus Bos. inventor* baldly engraved on it.

On Bruegel's return from Rome, Cock published the young artist's drawings of the countryside in a group of prints known as the *Large Landscape Series.* This was followed by a series of views of Brabant villages. Within two years Cock seems to have turned Bruegel loose on a whole series devoted to Boschlike grotesqueries and diabolic scenes. At the same time Bruegel was also turning out everyday subjects like harvesting, an occasional view of Antwerp's St. George's Gate and a collection of studies of sailing ships, which are still sold in European print shops. This phase of Bruegel's work culminated in his two greatest black and white creations—*The Seven Deadly Sins* (anger, sloth, lust, gluttony, avarice, pride and envy) and *The Virtues* (prudence, charity, justice, faith, hope, temperance and fortitude).

Since some of Bruegel's finest achievements as a painter were to be in landscape and since his earliest drawings were landscapes, it is tempting today to regard Hieronymus Cock as an exploiter who diverted the young Bruegel from his true bent toward landscape painting and wasted his creative energies by making him churn out busy drawings for the 16th Century equivalent of modern calendar art. Nothing could be further from the truth. Taken by themselves Bruegel's many drawings would have earned him an honored place in the history of art if he had never touched oils. Although the drawings now rest in the collections and museums of the world, seldom seen by the public—because drawings fade if exposed to the light—they are in relation to Bruegel's oil paintings what the supporting bulk of a submerged iceberg is to the snowy tip that shows above the surface.

It is impossible to set an exact date when Bruegel stopped working in black and white, mainly for Cock, and struck out on his own, almost exclusively as a painter. The best guess is 1563, the year Bruegel married and migrated from Antwerp to Brussels. But there can be no sharp line drawn, for Bruegel had begun painting as early as 1554 and, in general, every subject that he drew for Cock he also painted in oils for himself and his patrons. Consequently, the growth in range and subject and skill visible in Bruegel's drawings and prints is paralleled to a large extent by his progress in oil painting. *The Seven Deadly Sins,* for example, are clear artistic offshoots of Bosch. But *The Virtues,* executed shortly afterwards, are pure Bruegel; the human figures, although they are often lampoons and caricatures of real life, are never Boschian monsters—and they very much resemble the peasants and townsfolk used in Bruegel's later paintings. Similarly Bruegel's black and white world reflects the evolution visible in Bruegel's oils from scenes teeming with life to the presentation of a few massive dramatic figures, which show how well, in his own way, he had learned from Michelangelo.

In other respects, too, the world of prints and printmaking was a source of creative strength for Bruegel. As we have noted, he was a great borrower. He had a long reach, a sure hand and the skill to transform showy second-rate stuff into artistic triumphs that owed no creative debt to anyone. But to borrow something one must first have a chance to see it—and most oil paintings in the 16th Century were in private and often inaccessible collections. Through his involvement in the ever-growing flow of prints, Bruegel acquired a precise idea of the work done by painters North and South, past and present.

Bruegel put this knowledge to good use and before his death in 1569 became what amounted to a one-man Northern Renaissance in art. Some Flemish painters resisted the Italian influence to the point of ignoring it; others made too much use of it. In neither case did they develop their artistic individuality freely. Bruegel was the great exception. He learned from his Northern predecessors as much as from Michelangelo and the Mannerists. And he cross-bred painting subjects as no other painter in the 16th Century could. In ways that, as he grew older, became more individualized and less dependent on his models, he grafted the Renaissance's new historical subjects upon traditional Biblical illustrations and created commentary on the religious wars of his time. He took the minuscule countrysides of the Flemish Books of Hours and blew them up into the world's first great landscapes. This Bruegelian blending is the reason why

One of the most impressive and controversial publishing ventures undertaken during Bruegel's time was an eight volume polyglot Bible, which bore this handsomely engraved title page. Completed in Antwerp in 1573 under the supervision of Christopher Plantin—an outstanding pioneer in the early days of printing—and sponsored by Spain's King Philip II, the edition offered parallel texts in four languages: Hebrew, Greek, Latin and Chaldaic, an ancient Semitic language. At first the book was denounced by Catholic authorities as heretical and Judaistic and was banned by the Inquisition; but in 1580 it was finally approved and released to the public.

so few of his paintings can be classified into clearly separate categories, since often the official subject is merely an excuse for pursuing a divergent artistic aim. Proverb illustrations double as studies in everyday realism. Biblical illustrations become lovely winter scenes in which the Holy Family is barely discernible in a corner. Through it all Bruegel's great strength lay in his artistic contact with the Flemish past and with the sweaty, comic folkways of the Flemish people. His work on Hieronymus Cock's often earthy prints helped anchor him in native ground.

That Bruegel was able to experiment so boldly and still find patrons owes much to shifts that were taking place in the art world and to the bustling city that Antwerp had become in the 1550s. This fortified city on the muddy river Scheldt reached its peak as the commercial center of 16th Century Europe not long after Bruegel returned from Rome. It was in Antwerp that the first commercial insurance company was born, as well as the world's first international money market. The Antwerp waterfront served as the main port and clearing house for ships owned by the merchant-traders of the German Hanseatic League, coasting their way southwest from Hamburg and the Baltic toward Britanny, Spain and the Mediterranean. Gold from the Spanish possessions in the New World was traded here, as well as silver brought in barges down the Rhine from Germany, wine in wooden tuns from Bordeaux and bolts of cloth from the English ports of Bristol and Southampton. "It is wonderful," wrote the Italian diplomat and observer Ludovico Guicciardini, describing the foreign trading colonies that thrived in Antwerp, "to see such a concourse of men of so many different humors and qualities . . . so that without traveling abroad you can observe in a single town (and, if you so desire, imitate exactly) the ways of living customs of diverse nations."

Among the most desirable goods offered for sale in Flanders were oil paintings. A whole upper floor of the New Stock Exchange was reserved exclusively for the trade in works of art. Paintings sometimes sold so well, especially to Spain, the heaviest buyer, that they were sent off by the shipload. The demands of this large and lucrative market were met by the licensed members of the painters' guild—the medieval Guild of Saint Luke, named after the saint who in religious paintings is often shown painting the Virgin. At one time Antwerp could boast more licensed painters (some 300) than licensed butchers.

Although painters were still officially bound by medieval craft regulations, the impact of Renaissance prosperity was changing the art world—especially for men of genius like Bruegel. One kind of change is suggested by Van Mander's account of Bruegel and his merchant patron, Hans Franckert, going out together dressed as countryfolk so that Bruegel could make sketches of village fêtes as raw material for future paintings. That Bruegel could be so chummy with a patron, even in an anecdote, indicated a significant change in the artist's status in the 16th Century. From faithful and humble craftsmen employed by the Church and then docile decorators for princes, painters were slowly assuming the role of privileged individuals—whose skill at making pictures was sometimes compared to the original creation of the world. Hence the use of the word "divine" to describe Raphael. Hence, also, the 16th Century

Household objects used by wealthy burghers during Bruegel's time have a sturdy elegance. The handsome chair at top was carved from oak; its high, arched back is inlaid with other woods. The lion-topped wine tankard at center is of heavy pewter; the tumbler at bottom, inscribed in Latin, is glass with a metal base.

stories (many of them apocryphal) illustrating the reverence felt by great princes for great painters. The Emperor Charles V, it was whispered, once stooped to pick up a brush dropped by the Venetian master Titian. When shocked courtiers objected, Charles observed that while there would certainly be many courtiers, there was only one Titian.

The shift was slower in the North than in the South (as Albrecht Dürer emphasized when he wrote home from Venice to Germany in 1506 observing, "Here I am a gentleman, at home a nobody"). But change there was, and Bruegel was among those painters who apparently profited from it. Not that he grew rich and fashionable—he was never a court painter, never did a nude or a portrait. But he profited enough to become a painter with a recognized individual bent, sought out and paid high prices by a group of admirers who had the sense to let him do the things he wanted to do.

During his lifetime Bruegel seems to have been the favorite artist of four remarkable men. Hans Franckert, Abraham Ortelius and Niclaes Jonghelinck were not only patrons but also friends of the painter. The fourth, Cardinal Granvelle, was neither friend nor patron but a collector of Bruegel paintings both during and after the painter's lifetime. In the absence of biographical facts about Bruegel, the qualities of the first three patrons help define the kind of man the artist was. Hans Franckert has already appeared in Van Mander's account. But it is worth adding that he went to Antwerp from Germany and was a merchant cultivated enough to belong to the highly intellectual Chamber of Rhetoric in Antwerp. The patron who earned the most enduring reputation was map maker Abraham Ortelius. The first man of his time to correlate all the cartographic material turned up by explorers and map makers in his and earlier ages, the Antwerp cartographer issued it as a folio of world maps, inventively entitled *Theatrum Orbis Terrarum* (Theater of the World's Lands). Ortelius was a humanist intellectual who disapproved of violence whether practiced by Catholic or Protestant. He owned at least one Bruegel painting and counted the painter as a personal friend. When Bruegel died Ortelius mourned him with a formal printed epitaph, which praised Bruegel for being true to nature and for painting men not fashionably, but honestly.

Bruegel's richest patron was Niclaes Jonghelinck. It was he who inadvertently provided posterity with the greatest single collection of Bruegel paintings that has survived until today. In 1565 Jonghelinck commissioned Bruegel to do a series of paintings showing landscapes at various seasons. The pictures—the only works of Bruegel that we know to have been done on commission—were splendid. In the following year Jonghelinck, caught in a credit squeeze, found himself forced to pledge his whole art collection to the city of Antwerp. The inventory shows that he owned 16 Bruegels, 20 paintings by Frans Floris and one original by Albrecht Dürer—the collection was valued at the large sum of 16,000 florins. Eventually acquired by the Habsburg Archduke Ernst as a gift from the city of Antwerp when he was made governor of Flanders in 1594, the Bruegel pictures became a part of the Habsburg family collection that now hangs in the Vienna Kunsthistorisches Museum.

Through Cardinal Granvelle, an ambitious career churchman who served for more than five years as the hated president of the Netherlands' Council of State and was Philip II's political agent in the Low Countries, we may examine another facet of Bruegel's life and work—the relation of the painter and his paintings to the tragic political and religious history of his times.

Antoine Perrenot Cardinal de Granvelle, first comes to notice as an inveterate Bruegel collector in 1576 when the Spanish mercenary forces, which burned and sacked Antwerp as part of Philip's reprisal against the Protestant rebellion, also made off with most of the cardinal's Antwerp art collection, containing three Bruegels. But Granvelle's personality, power and reputation have also touched off speculation about Bruegel's politics and religion—especially in connection with Bruegel's sudden migration from Antwerp to Brussels after his marriage in 1563. Van Mander, as we have seen, says that the move reflected the shrewdness of the painter's mother-in-law who thought Breugel should turn over a new leaf and make a clean break with his attractive former housekeeper; but historians and critics tend to view the suggestion as flimsy and frivolous.

Instead, they turn to history. Antwerp was a hotbed of Anabaptist and Calvinist agitation. Even as early as 1563 the Catholic establishment held trials and public executions of heretics to counter Protestant resistance. These actions, instead of ending clandestine preaching by Protestants to crowds in the countryside, gave rise to threats to steal prisoners from the Inquisition by force and to launch a full-scale assault on Catholic churches and religious orders in Antwerp—all of which violence actually did occur in the following years. According to one line of historical argument, Bruegel got out of Antwerp just in time to avoid civil disorder.

Thus far, the argument is probably correct. But the next step in the argument involves not Bruegel's common sense but his religious and political loyalties. Why, it has been asked, if he was a good Catholic, did he have to flee—as so many men known to be suspect by the authorities were forced to do? Wasn't he instead a not-so-secret partisan of Protestantism? There is no answer. But there is a rebuttal. Why should a celebrated painter, if he were suspect by Catholic authorities, move from Antwerp, where much of the population had Protestant leanings, and place himself openly in Brussels, the strongly Catholic capital of the Spanish Low Countries? Besides, it is added, Granvelle collected Bruegel's paintings. Granvelle was Philip's man; and he was so touchy about respect for Catholic Church authority that he once accused Flemish noblemen of treason merely because they dressed their servants in red cowls —the cardinal asserted that because the cowls resembled cardinals' robes they reflected disrespect for the Church. Would such a man have hung on his palace walls pictures by a painter suspected of heresy?

The arguments are circular. But they put us squarely in front of one of the most fascinating questions about the world of Pieter Bruegel: how far do his pictures reflect the enormities that went on all about him? And, in doing so, to what extent do they reveal the man? Since Bruegel himself left no answers, they must be sought in a careful comparison of his art and the history of his times.

The Vices and Virtues

In his late twenties, when he was still little known as a painter, Pieter Bruegel began a job that launched his career with unexpected speed. He became a designer of engravings for Hieronymus Cock, Antwerp's leading publisher, at the House of the Four Winds. Under Cock's supervision, Bruegel's superb drawings were copied by craftsmen on copper plates and printed and sold by the thousands throughout Europe.

Bruegel prepared many subjects for the engravers, including townscapes, ships, landscapes and religious scenes. Among his most popular prints were two complementary series, *The Seven Deadly Sins* and *The Virtues,* selections from which are reproduced on the following pages. In each a central allegorical figure stands for the theme. In the *Sins* represented here—gluttony, anger and pride—this figure is surrounded by a battery of fantastic creatures, some of which are obviously inspired by Bosch. Sometimes these grotesque creations symbolize the sin they most often practice—the insatiable humanoid windmill in *Gluttony,* for example; occasionally they are being punished for it. In *The Virtues*—hope, justice and temperance are shown—the central figure stands amid a crowd of humans acting in a righteous fashion. But at times these paragons carry virtue to the point of foolish excess, and in a canny moral commentary Bruegel shows some of them behaving with so fanatical a zeal that it amounts to sinfulness.

The nightmarish monsters who inhabit Bruegel's *Sin* series, published in 1558, give way to a more human representation in *The Virtues,* which were produced two years later. But he combined the two styles in a transitional print, *Patience,* which is neither a vice nor a major virtue.

Bruegel Invent.

PATIENTIA.

H Cock · excude · 1557.

Patience Chained to a block and clutching a crucifix, a long-suffering woman endures the sorry spectacle of sinning beasts and distorted humans surrounding her.

GVLA.

SPES

BRVEGEL. INV.

H. cock excu.

P. Brueghel. Inuentor.

IRA

H. Cock excude. Cum gratia et priuilegio. 1558.

JUSTICE Blindfolded for impartiality, this gowned figure does not see the awful tortures committed in the name of truth-finding, correction and good example.

SVPERBIA.

.P. breughel Inuentor.

Cock excud cum priuileg 1558

Temperance   Surrounded by the useful and creative arts of which the restrained man is capable, a bridled (self-controlled) lady balances the clock upon her head.

IV

Parables and Parallels in the Bible

Bruegel's *Adoration of the Kings*—he painted three different versions of the scene—reveals a mixture of styles. The lumpish figures and rough faces of the common people—including Joseph to whom an attendant whispers —show Bruegel's realism. But the stately pose of the Virgin and the elongated posture of the Christ Child reveal the influence of the Italian Renaissance—perhaps the work of Michelangelo—which Bruegel knew from his trip to Italy.

The Adoration of the Kings, 1564

During the crowning creative epoch of Bruegel's life the conflict in the Netherlands between Catholics and Protestants, between the Spanish king and the local nobility grew more bitter, progressing from suspicion and terror to bloodshed and open war. Bruegel did not record these political and religious crises directly in his art. Of necessity in such dangerous times, his treatment had to be oblique and metaphoric—most often confined to Biblical subjects with double meanings. Yet many of Bruegel's most powerful and touching pictures reflect the plight and preoccupations of his anguished fellow countrymen during the dark years between 1560 and 1569.

The actual revolt of the Low Countries against Spanish rule did not begin until the 1560s. But on October 25, 1555, the coming tragedy had a dramatic prologue—the abdication of Charles V. On that day nobles from all over the Netherlands gathered for the ceremony in the grand salon of the Imperial palace in Brussels. Officially they had been invited to witness the ritual bequeathing of the Netherlands to Charles's son, Philip of Spain. At the same time, had they known, they were being treated to a remarkable historic tableau in which all the great actors who would soon take part in the bloody division of the Low Countries were ranged together on stage.

At stage center sat the Emperor Charles, fittingly clad in black, weeping as he said goodbye. Below him knelt Philip, a full-fleshed, blond prince of 28, with a curly beard and a plump Habsburg lower lip. For support the Emperor leaned on a dark young nobleman with short-cropped hair and beard. This was Prince William of Orange. Raised in the Brussels court as Charles's ward—virtually as his son—William was still, in 1555, a loyal friend and soldier of the Empire. Eventually Philip's harsh rule would transform him from Spain's strongest supporter in the Low Countries into Spain's bitterest enemy, a tireless and courageous rebel leader who, more than any other man, was responsible for the rise of the new Dutch nation.

Behind Charles stood a figure in ecclesiastical garb, Antoine Perrenot de Granvelle, the Bishop of Arras. This ambitious prelate's part in the abdication ceremony did not come until the awkward moment when young Philip, after gracefully accepting his new lands and responsibilities with a few well-chosen words in Spanish, found himself obliged to apologize to the assembled nobles because it was not possible for him to express his love for the Netherlands in any tongue that his new subjects spoke—not, as he said, "in French, and even less in Flemish." In some embarrassment he turned to Bishop Granvelle and asked him to read the royal acceptance speech in French. "Please hear him," Philip reminded the nobles, "as you would hear me."

Dutifully they did so. And Granvelle, obediently reading the prepared text, symbolically performed a service that he was soon to perform on a much larger and more sinister scale. For it was Granvelle, acting as Philip's principal spokesman in the Netherlands after the monarch returned to Madrid, who had to implement the King's policies against his angry subjects in the distant Netherlands.

The last figure of great importance standing near Charles was Ferdinand Alvarez de Toledo, the Duke of Alba, a bearded hawk-faced soldier who was to wield Philip's avenging sword in the Low Countries when revolt actually broke out. Netherlanders came to know him as Black Alba, partly because he customarily dressed in black, mainly because they believed the Duke's heart was the color of his costume.

From a historical viewpoint, what now seems most significant about Charles's abdication is the fact that in bequeathing the Netherlands to Philip, Charles was saddling Spain with a burden of responsibilities that would soon exceed her natural capabilities and concerns. The Netherlands, lost in northern fogs, exposed on one flank to heretical England, vulnerable on the other to Protestant Germany, lay half a continent away from Madrid. Spain's normal spheres of interest had already been fixed to the south in the Mediterranean and westward toward the Americas where conquistadors were, even then, carving out a new Hispanic world. From a modern perspective, it seems almost inevitable that the Netherlands should have caused Spain nothing but trouble from the time of Philip's succession.

But what struck Philip's audience as most significant was the chilling fact that their new King did not speak their language. French was the tongue of courtiers in the Low Countries. Dutch, derived from German, was the tongue of the people. Philip knew neither. He was a hostile foreigner and an absentee monarch with no geographic or emotional claims to his subjects' loyalty.

Charles V, admittedly, had often ruled the Netherlands from as far away as Madrid. He had, besides, set in motion many of the policies that Philip was to follow. Charles's attempts to suppress Protestantism in the Low Countries had led to a succession of antiheretical edicts, culminating in the so-called Edict of Blood, which set death as the penalty for all heresies. Characteristically, however, Charles was too busy fighting the Turks and the French ever to see to it that the edicts were enforced to the letter. Far from making Netherlanders feel like the playthings of a foreign ruler, the fact that Charles had far-flung responsibilities as Emperor gave them the illusion—to a large extent justified—that the Netherlands was the center of Europe. Wherever he went and whatever he did Charles remained *their* prince, born in Ghent and raised in Brussels, a man who spoke their language and knew their ways.

Philip, the Netherlanders sensed, was something else again. Charles had been a popular leader on the battlefield. Philip learned early that in combat he was afflicted by diarrhea and wisely preferred to conduct his campaigns from a desk in Madrid. Charles was fond of the Netherlands, easygoing with its nobles. Philip hated the Netherlands and looked upon its 17 provinces—each one with a slightly different form of local government—as a disorderly challenge to his powers as an administrator. In Philip's eyes the independence and traditional rights of the nobility in the Low Countries were little more than an encouragement to treason. Even worse, from Philip's viewpoint, the Netherlands had become a hotbed of Protestant heresy. In the wake of Lutheranism and Anabaptism, Calvinism was now stalking the land. Unlike the other two sects, Calvin's muscular doctrine was a faith that came with a built-in political threat at all levels: energetic Calvinist church elders, wherever they found a foothold, expected to direct not only the spiritual but also the temporal affairs of their congregations.

Shocked by these conditions, the new monarch of the Low Countries decided he must unite the provinces, cut the power of the nobles and ruthlessly stamp out the heresy. For a few years he was kept busy pursuing the military and political affairs initiated by his father. But in 1559 Charles died, and Philip was free to act on his own.

To wipe out the blight of heresy he decreed that the Edict of Blood be enforced to the utmost. He chose his half-sister, Margaret of Parma, as his regent in the Netherlands to rule in his name. But as a further check on the influence of the great lords he appointed Bishop Granvelle, soon to be made a cardinal, as both president of the Netherlands Council of State and chief of the Council's powerful Executive Committee. The latter, a small group that handled most of the Council's policy-making, was staffed mainly by nobles subservient to Philip's will. Since most of these lords were *stadhouders,* or governors, of their provinces, and since their political power—where it concerned the Netherlands as a whole—was exercised through the Council, Philip was in effect making Granvelle ruler of the Netherlands.

The monarch's master strategy for reorganizing the Netherlands Church called for more bishops, and more loyal ones; smaller and better-organized episcopal sees. The plan also included the gradual replacement of the hodgepodge of local clergy—many of them the younger sons of great Dutch and Flemish families—by Spanish career priests, appointed by the Crown.

Like much of what Philip proposed, the plans were administratively sound on paper, but difficult to put into practice. The bishoprics were never fully reorganized; local resistance to this and other programs proved too great. In a land where for years trade had been amicably carried on in half a dozen tongues and where, at least in cities like Antwerp, foreigners were fully accepted, the use of the Spanish language and the presence of Spanish administrators soon became unbearable. The presence

A magnificent portrait of Philip II by Titian, Bruegel's great Venetian contemporary, shows the future Spanish King at the age of 26, three years before his coronation in 1556. The artist captured Philip's regal bearing and revealed a hint of his unyielding nature— an uncanny portent of future blunders that led Spain into constant conflict with France and England and plunged the Netherlands into a savage civil war.

in the Netherlands of 3,000 Spanish soldiers, left over from a campaign against France in 1558, stirred the people to fear and rage. Philip's requests for money and for Netherlandish troops to serve his policies—to both of which as legal sovereign he was completely entitled—were looked upon almost as a national affront, even before the concept of a Dutch nation properly existed.

Nourished by Philip's relentless hostility, Calvinism soon became something very like a national cause. Protestant preaching had long been banned in the cities; after 1560 Calvinists and other Protestant ministers began preaching outdoors in the country, giving so-called "hedge sermons." Elsewhere the increase in public executions kept pace with the growing Protestant agitation, and the death toll sickened nobles and populace alike. Churchmen involved in heresy trials—and executioners too—often were in danger of popular violence. "It is not we who put you to death," one troubled sheriff apologized to a condemned prisoner in 1564, "but the King's decree." The same year, in Antwerp, crowds stoned the executioners at the burning of a heretic. In the meantime streams of petitions were being sent off to Spain pleading for religious moderation and the removal of Granvelle and the Spanish troops from the Low Countries.

To Philip this was outrageous disloyalty. At first he refused to stir—then gave in only when it was too late. The troops were finally withdrawn, but they had already been there long enough to rouse the country thoroughly. Granvelle was retired in 1564, but not before he had made himself thoroughly unpopular—in part for allegedly plotting, on Philip's behalf, to have William of Orange murdered.

In the late spring of 1566 the anti-Protestant edicts were slightly modified—not by Philip, but through a compromise worked out by the frightened regent, Margaret, and leading Netherlandish nobles. They all grasped, as Philip did not, that the populace could not be controlled otherwise. But even this concession to religious pressures came too late. Throughout the Netherlands, and especially in the northern provinces, Calvinist extremists had been steadily at work. Now the temper of the country was such that it would willingly accept nothing short of complete religious freedom.

The storm broke in the sweltering summer of 1566. Catholic churchmen were driven into the streets. In a score of Flemish cities crowds of Calvinist agitators and city rabble assaulted nunneries and beat up monks. In a period of three weeks mobs sacked 400 Catholic churches, destroying holy images, scattering relics, slashing and burning altar paintings, drinking Communion wine and, according to one observer, feeding pieces of the Host to pet parrots. "Coming into Oure Lady Church," a shocked English diplomat wrote in 1566, "yt looked like hell wher were above 1,000 torches brannyng and syche a noise as yf heven and erth had gone together with fallyng of images and fallyng down of costly works."

The public outrages committed by both sides were matched by a strange, private political struggle being carried on between Philip and William of Orange. However much William protested (and showed) his loyalty, both Philip and Granvelle assumed he was a secret enemy. He was, after all, rich, powerful and popular, and he had Protestant family connections in Germany. Even more incriminating was the fact that he steadily urged moderation upon the King. Margaret of Parma was not sure where William stood, and sometimes William was not even sure himself. For years he struggled to balance his duties as a prince responsible for the well-being of his own people in the provinces of Holland and Zeeland and as a vassal responsible to Philip. Philip was his legal lord, the legitimate monarch of the Low Countries. Both as a noble and as a protégé of Charles V, William owed allegiance to Philip—which included not only the right to give sound counsel but also the duty to obey even if the advice was ignored.

By conviction William was a conservative. He cared little for religion but believed profoundly in law and order, and he hated the excesses of cruelty that religious zeal, on whatever side, so often produced. For this reason he steadily resisted Philip's inquisitorial war on heresy. "To see a man burnt for doing as he thought right," he once told the regent, "harms the people, for this is a matter of conscience." But William equally disliked the martyr-seeking zeal of the Calvinists, and in 1566 he sent his own troops to put down a threatened revolt in Antwerp and disperse the crowds of idol-smashers. So, troubled by his dilemma, William urged moderation on both sides, and took neither. (For his own restraint and ability to keep his counsel he was to become known as William the Silent.) He maintained his uneasy neutrality from 1560 until 1566, when events occurred that forced him finally to commit himself to the cause of rebellion.

Granvelle's departure left the regent, Margaret, as Philip's chief agent in the Low Countries, and she had neither the skill nor the stomach to administer his policies. She rode well, sported a small mustache and, as one court flatterer remarked, looked more like a man in woman's dress than a woman. But she was no expert at political maneuvering, was bewildered by the hostility of the Netherlandish nobility and completely unable to cope with the country's growing unrest and disorder. She was particularly nervous about a revolutionary band of extremist lords known as the Confederation of Nobles and was once chided by a courtier who said, "What, Madame! Are you frightened of these beggars?" He did not noticeably bolster Margaret's will, but he inadvertently provided the opposition, high and low, with a popular nickname: *les Gueux*—the Beggars. *Vivent les Gueux* swiftly became a rallying cry for members of the Confederation who stalked about wearing beggars' traditional foxtails and wooden bowls.

When the anti-Church rioting took place in 1566, Margaret's pleas were the loudest in the chorus that came from all over the Netherlands begging Philip to come to Brussels and see for himself what his austere policies had wrought. Characteristically, Philip delayed. Then, after finally agreeing to come, he made no plans for a journey. Instead, he secretly commissioned the Duke of Alba to gather an army of 20,000 men, march to the Netherlands, relieve Margaret as regent and crush both heresy and rebellion. It was this step that transformed William of Orange from a vacillating vassal into a national revolutionary leader. Learning of King Philip's decision, he escaped to Germany and began trying to raise an army of liberation.

Because of the longstanding hostility between France and Spain, Alba could not follow a direct overland route from Madrid to Brussels. Instead, he had to sail his troops to Italy and then march them up through the Alps to reach Flanders. As his richly equipped army wound like a slow serpent through the passes of the lower Alps, news of its coming sent tremors through the courts of Europe. In the imagination of the Netherlanders, it loomed like approaching doom.

Alba reached Brussels in August, 1567. Methodical and energetic, the Duke quickly established a Spanish court around him in Brussels and set up a special body of Spanish judges to study treason and heresy. (Officially called the Council of Troubles, it became known as the Council of Blood.) Loosing his soldiers on the countryside, Alba swiftly seized, tried and put to death as traitors or heretics large numbers of Dutch and Flemish citizens. In 1568 he handily scattered the ragtag forces that had been hastily assembled by William. But William himself escaped, and resistance lingered on.

William was to return in 1574 with another army and succeed in breaking a long siege by the Spanish of the city of Leiden, thus ensuring the continued existence of an all-but-independent collection of rebel provinces in the north, which would eventually become the new country of Holland. But that culminating event was far in the future. William, Alba, even Philip himself would be long dead before the 80 years of bloodshed that the King's policies had unleashed came to an end.

Pieter Bruegel saw no more than the very beginning of that long war —he died just two years after Alba first arrived in Brussels with his troops. Yet the war and the persecutions that led up to it served as background to the mature years of his life. Since he was a painter inclined toward the secular rather than the sacred, it was only natural that the events about him were reflected in his art. Given the age in which he painted, it was only natural, too, that the vehicle he used was Biblical illustration.

For the people of Bruegel's time, history and the Bible and the trials of everyday life were inextricably mingled. The Bible was accepted as truthful history, a chronicle of the remote past in which, for hundreds of years, man had been trained to find uplifting and didactic parallels with the present. Individuals in moments of anguish sought encouragement and solace from the example of New and Old Testament characters: in the stubborn uprightness of Job, the gentle grief of Mary mourning Christ, the disciplined heroism of Joshua. Quite naturally, too, they also saw parallels between Biblical characters and the great public figures of their own age, and compared the political troubles of the present with those of the past. The Emperor Charles V, for example, as the perennial defender of Catholic Europe against Protestant heretics and the pagan hordes of Suleiman the Magnificent, was frequently compared by Catholics to King David, the Biblical defender of God's chosen people against the Philistines and Amalekites.

That it seemed logical to Bruegel to dress Biblical characters in con-

GRAPHISCHE SAMMLUNG ALBERTINA, VIENNA

temporary costumes reveals a 16th Century attitude toward the past that is not easily shared today. Unlike 20th Century man, Bruegel's country-men were not separated from preceding ages by an abyss of feeling or an acute awareness of intervening technological growth. For them, the past was a time, not very different from the present, when the common folk must have lived much as they were living in the 16th Century. They had only a vague knowledge of geography and a murky notion of whatever centuries-long changes in costume and custom had taken place. Unlike us, they felt little sense of anachronism when confronted by the spectacle of St. Paul riding with a modern army through the Alps, or Golgotha transported to a suburb of Ghent. Anyone painting in Bruegel's time could count on this. He could also count on an audience that was alertly tuned to read into any Biblical scene possible symbolic comment on the age in which he lived.

At the same time, Northern painters were growing more and more worldly in their ways of handling the Bible. In the first place, the Flemish fondness for realistic detail was being emphasized more and more, to the point where Biblical incidents were often subordinated to general scenes of everyday affairs. This was particularly true of Bruegel, whose artistic bent lay not in the pious glorification of God but in the delineation of impious man. In *The Carrying of the Cross (pages 108-111)*, he all but bur-ied the figure of Christ with His burden in the jostling crowd. The artist

Bruegel's father-in-law, Pieter Coeck van Aelst, was also an important artist. During a visit to Constantinople in 1533 he produced a series of woodcuts that are especially valued for historical research. This one depicts Sultan Suleiman I parading with his retinue. A year before Pieter Coeck's visit, Suleiman had been defeated near Vienna by Charles V. The Sultan is preceded by archers, flanked by two bodyguards swinging clubs and followed by two chamberlains on horseback. The caryatid in Turkish garb at the extreme right was the artist's device for separating the narrative panels in his prints, which were published in a continuous band.

95

did the same thing in a painting called *Adoration of the Kings in the Snow*, executed late in his career, in 1564. Two earlier Bruegel *Adorations* had been entirely traditional, with the Virgin Mary, the Infant, the Magi, in conventional, prominent positions. The third painting is radically different. It shows a beautiful Flemish village in winter, with great soft flakes of snow spiraling down on a shuffle of dogs, donkeys and countryfolk. Only by searching can a viewer finally find the shadowy corner where the small, shrouded figure of the Virgin and the adoring Kings can just be made out.

Besides this inclination to de-emphasize Biblical incident, Northern painters in their treatment of the Bible were beginning to respond to the Italian Renaissance conviction that scenes from history could be suitably uplifting subjects for art. Early Flemish Bible illustration had once been largely devoted to scenes like the Nativity, the Crucifixion and the Descent from the Cross. Slowly it gravitated more toward those episodes from the Old and New Testaments that are concerned less with sacred passion than with anecdote. Moreover, the episodes chosen were often ones with which contemporary parallels could be drawn. A number of Bruegel's best-known paintings—the *Tower of Babel, Conversion of St. Paul, Suicide of King Saul,* and *Massacre of the Innocents*—clearly document both developments.

The Tower of Babel not surprisingly became a favorite subject in Flanders, a land that traded in many tongues and that was resentfully having still another language, Spanish, imposed upon it. Ostensibly the tower belongs to a special type of Scriptural story aimed at explaining contradictions that tend to puzzle Bible students—in this case, how it happens that there are so many different languages when everyone in the world is supposedly descended from members of Noah's immediate family. Allegorically, however, the tower is a monumental warning against a particular form of pride, which Philip, with his grandiose plans for unifying the Netherlands, exemplified—the pride of ambitious human beings who seek to organize the world around them.

According to the Bible story, the descendants of Noah in Babylon set out to build a tower high enough to challenge heaven. They also erected a brick city intended, like Philip's Netherlands, to serve as an administrative center of social cohesion and union. When Jehovah observed this prideful effort, he caused the people to speak in many tongues. Suddenly, bricklayers could not give orders to workers. The King's overseers (like Granvelle) could not get anyone to obey their orders. The entire work force fragmented into warring little knots of "foreigners," and soon the whole immense work came to a halting end.

Earlier painters in illustrating this story tended to make the tower a fairly simple structure. Bruegel's *Tower (pages 9-12)* is much more: both a symbolic portrait of the Netherlands and a confirmed pessimist's history of human society. King Nimrod, popularly accepted as the tower's princely builder, stands small in the foreground, just another petty bigwig interfering with the work in progress. It doesn't really matter, though, for the mountainous structure behind him will clearly never be finished. If the tower unmistakably represents man's works in general, shown in all their pip-squeak sweat and folly, the countryside it inhabits is just as unmistakably the Netherlands.

What is true of the *Tower of Babel* is also true of Bruegel's other Biblical paintings. Sometimes they seem to be directly linked to specific events, and sometimes they merely mirror metaphorically the preoccupations of his contemporaries. Precisely at the moment when Netherlanders were turning their minds, fearfully or gladly, to the approach of the Duke of Alba's expeditionary force, Bruegel painted his *Conversion of St. Paul (pages 104-105)*. The Biblical episode, which describes the conversion of an anti-Christian soldier, is transplanted from a dusty road leading from Jerusalem to Damascus and set down in an Alpine pass where Saul, when felled by a blinding light from God, is leading an up-to-date Renaissance army on the march.

In 1562, when Bruegel was painting the *Suicide of King Saul*, his countrymen were just becoming aware of the long, now-you-trust-him, now-you-don't duel between William the Silent and Philip II—a duel that, for anyone who had read I and II Kings, could hardly fail to suggest King Saul's alternating feud and friendship with his reluctant rival for power and popularity, the young David. Similarly, Bruegel painted the *Massacre of the Innocents (page 103)* at a time when the Low Countries were every day witnessing scenes of political and religious repression. In the Bible story King Herod, hearing of the birth of a new Messiah in Bethlehem, ordered his soldiers to kill all the baby boys in the town. Bruegel situated his *Massacre of the Innocents* in a snowbound Brabant village where the bitter northern cold seems to cut as cruelly as the swords of the brutal soldiery—dressed in the red cloaks of the Walloon cavalry, often used as police troops by the regent, Margaret.

Allthis is no coincidence. These paintings unquestionably reflect Bruegel's awareness of the political turmoil of his time. But they also confront the viewer, once again, with the tantalizing question: did Bruegel take sides, and if so, which one? Do the clear parallels that exist between Bruegel's paintings and contemporary history carry a personal and partisan political commentary?

The tempting assumption is that they do. The popular choice, naturally, is to make Bruegel a secret partisan of Calvinism, a subtle propagandist for William and the Netherlands, a skillful adversary of Philip and Spain. History, after all, has cast Philip and Alba as the villains of the piece.

Unhappily, the evidence is pretty evenly balanced both for and against this assumption. As a friend of the cartographer Abraham Ortelius, for example, Bruegel belonged to the intellectual world of Antwerp, the greatest stronghold of Calvinism in the Low Countries. Yet the intellectual world of the city was also deeply influenced by the teachings of Erasmus, who, as the Reformation grew progressively more violent, preached moderation and refused to take sides. Again, Bruegel chose to move to Brussels in 1563, just before a series of anti-Catholic outbursts in Antwerp. But, as we have seen, no one can be sure whether he did it to escape punishment for Protestant leanings, or simply to avoid having to take sides at all.

The Biblical story of the Tower of Babel attracted early artists at least partly because it served as a fitting illustration of human ambition gone astray. In the early 15th Century manuscript illumination at the top, from the Bedford Book of Hours, the artist created a fanciful structure of modest size and animated his scene with busy workmen. Below is a more ambitious tower complete with a panoramic landscape. It was executed for the Grimani Breviary about 1515. Bruegel's *Tower* appears on pages 9-12.

The paintings themselves are extremely equivocal. Take the *Conversion of St. Paul,* for instance. If the army shown in the Alps is Alba's—and such an idea was bound to suggest itself to Bruegel's public—all sorts of parallels between St. Paul on the road to Damascus and the Duke en route to Brussels immediately leap to mind. Before his conversion, St. Paul, as Saul the Benjamite, was a fiercely orthodox Jew actively engaged in putting down Christianity, then viewed as a dangerously heretical sect; Alba was setting out to suppress the Calvinist heresy in the Netherlands. Saul was bound on an anti-Christian mission when the thunderbolt struck him down on the road to Damascus. "Saul, Saul," the Lord's voice said to him out of the dust and blinding light, "why persecutest thou me?" What could seem more logical than that Pieter Bruegel, using an unexceptional Biblical subject as cover, was indirectly putting the same question; that he was, symbolically, praying that the cruel Duke, like the cruel Saul before him, might be converted to the true religion (in this case Protestantism) before he reached his own Damascus, in this case Brussels?

But another interpretation is just as possible. The Council of Trent, initiated by Charles V, was intended to mobilize the demoralized Catholic Church for the Counter Reformation. Philip's aim in the Low Countries was partly to reclaim for Rome ecclesiastical ground dangerously riddled with heresy. "Why talk about 1,700 put to death, many of them vile animals such as the Anabaptists," Philip was to write, defending Alba's inquisitorial procedures in Brussels, "and not write about the thousands who would die in the Netherlands if they succeeded in transplanting the Huguenot wars there as they wish to do!"

One of the prime aims of the Counter Reformation, as well as one of the dramatic preoccupations of Catholic thought just at that time, was the mounting of a militant effort to convert heretics and heathens. The notable example of the age was Ignatius of Loyola, a tough and brilliant Spanish soldier whose conversion from a profligate adventurer to a man of vigorous piety had led in 1546 to the founding of the Society of Jesus, a kind of spiritual Marine Corps for the war on Protestantism. Could not Bruegel have painted his *Conversion of St. Paul* to express a pious Catholic hope that the troops of Alba, as part of the Counter Reformation forces, would meet with many "conversions," when they engaged the Calvinist heretics in the Netherlands? Bruegel, after all, was admired by Cardinal Granvelle; he stood well enough with the authorities of Catholic Brussels to have been commissioned by them to do a series of pictures (probably never completed and now lost) of the construction of the new Brussels-Antwerp canal.

This equivocal quality in Bruegel's Biblical paintings, where the ostensible piety of the subject might easily have served as protective camouflage for a man dealing in double meanings, is also true of the artist's non-Biblical treatments of contemporary subjects. The best example is *The Cripples (pages 132-133).* Painted in 1568, this picture of maimed beggars clearly assumes that Netherlanders who see it will be reminded of *les Gueux,* with their begging bowls and foxtails, who only two years earlier had been nationally known symbols of the resistance to Spain. But

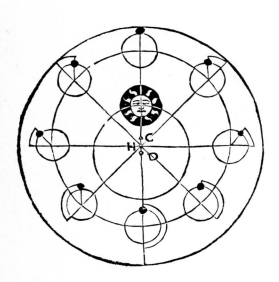

The astronomical system taught by the Second Century astronomer Claudius Ptolemy was based on the belief that the earth lies at the center of the universe and that the sun and the planets move around it. In this model of Saturn's orbit around the earth, Ptolemy explains the observable variation in the distance between the earth and Saturn *(black dots on small circles),* which is closer to the earth at the bottom of the diagram than at the top. He thought that Saturn, as well as orbiting the earth, rotates in a smaller circle (an epicycle) around a point whose center in its turn revolves around point C just alongside the earth (point D). Ptolemy's theories were challenged in 1543, when Bruegel was still in his teens, by the Polish mathematician Nicolas Copernicus, whose system *(opposite page)* showed the earth and planets revolving around the sun. Copernicus' ideas were heresy to the Church, which insisted that the earth, as the home of man, God's principal creation, was the center of God's universe.

looking at the picture it is impossible to decide whether Bruegel was pro-beggar or anti-beggar. What he created is one of the unloveliest little paintings ever. The begging cripples, as one critic remarked, look "as if a family of poisonous mushrooms had grown out of the damp ground in a remote corner." To intend such a painting as a symbol of covert sympathy with the *Gueux* would be like using a portrait of Dracula to encourage blood-bank donations.

Bruegel's reticence about revealing himself in his art is not confined to political matters. There is scarcely a hint of personal feeling in any of his paintings and never any appeal for the viewer's sympathy. Bruegel's cripples, his beggars, his blind men tumbling into a ditch are just there, part of the world as it is. This, Bruegel seems to say, is the world. This is man. Take him or leave him if you can. Of all his Biblical paintings there is only one that, by the nature of its subject, by the savagery of its treatment and by some of the details it includes, seems at all to engage Bruegel's personal feeling and so situate him in the partisan political spectrum of his time. That is the *Massacre of the Innocents,* a horrifying picture, which has led to a fascinating pictorial controversy.

Actually, Bruegel painted two pictures of the massacre, and, as he treated it, the subject made such an appalling onslaught upon viewers' sensibilities that in the 17th Century one version was touched up to hide the flesh and faces of the babies who are being killed. It is the untouched version *(page 103)* that raises disputes today. For in it appears, at the head of the armor-clad cavalry in the background, a bearded man all in black. The picture is undated, and that is at the core of the controversy. Educated guesses as to its date range anywhere from 1564 to 1567, the year when the Duke of Alba first entered the Low Countries. If it could be proved that the *Massacre* was painted *after* Alba came and that Bruegel (and not some later partisan Dutch painter) painted in the black figure to look like Alba, there would be little doubt of Bruegel's meaning.

But it is unlikely that proof to support this interpretation will be found. Far more likely is the assumption that Bruegel took no sides at all; that, like the philosopher Erasmus, he disapproved of all violence committed in the name of Christianity, by Calvinists and Catholics alike.

We know that one of Bruegel's close friends, Ortelius, agreed with Erasmus about the tragic futility of all causes bloodily pursued. When the philosopher wrote, "Let others affect martyrdom, for myself I am unworthy of the honor," he was not expressing fear but ironic disapproval. The same disapproval was expressed in a different way by Ortelius. In the Netherlands' struggle Ortelius was suspected of Protestant leanings. He avoided martyrdom by keeping his opinions to himself and finally by slipping across the channel to England to weather the fiercest years of political storm. He made his view clear enough, however, in letters kept secret at the time. "We live in a very disordered time, which we have little hope of seeing soon improved," he wrote. "The patient will soon be entirely prostrate, being threatened with so many and various illnesses, as the Catholic evil, the *Gueux* fever and the Huguenot dysentery." Or, to put it in other words, a pox on both your houses. Pieter Bruegel probably agreed with him.

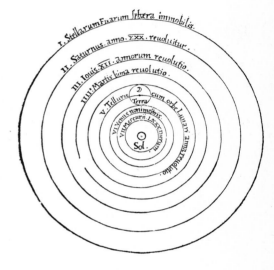

Copernicus' system firmly placed the sun at the center of the universe with the planets, including earth *(Terra),* orbiting it in concentric circles. Copernicus, moreover, recognized that the moon is a satellite not of the sun but of earth—and indicated the fact with a half-moon symbol and tiny circle. Copernicus' explanation was published with a preface by a Lutheran minister, who softened its impact by asserting that it was pure speculation. As such, the Roman Catholic Church did not at first object to the great astronomer's discoveries. But when a brilliant Italian religious philosopher, Giordano Bruno, using Copernicus' ideas and their theological implications as a starting point, began preaching the existence of a limitless universe teeming with inhabited planets, he was imprisoned, then burnt at the stake. In 1616 a papal edict banned as heretical the notion that the earth moves around the sun. Though the ban was not officially lifted until 1822, Copernicus' heliocentric theories had by then been accepted everywhere.

The Holy Land Transplanted

Around the year 1558, when he was in his early thirties, Bruegel seems to have begun devoting less time to drawing and more time to painting. Throughout his lifetime, Bruegel's pictures—concerned with sinful men, saintly deeds and Bible stories—reflected the religious and moral preoccupations of his age. But his turn of mind and eye increasingly inclined him toward the worldly and satiric, an inclination in tune with the changing times, since flourishing trade and the effects of Renaissance learning were broadening taste in the Netherlands. With this double impetus toward sophistication, Bruegel was soon using Biblical scenes as settings for landscapes and the realistic portrayal of everyday life and in moralizing on and satirizing human folly.

Bruegel's age was wracked by religious struggles between Catholics and the new Protestant sects and by political conflicts between Spain and the Low Countries. Like many of his contemporaries, Bruegel transported events from Biblical Judaea to his own time and country —as the cruel detail opposite illustrates. In 1567 Flanders was occupied by Spanish troops under the Duke of Alba, who acted thereafter both as de facto ruler and merciless represser of heresy. Many of Bruegel's religious paintings contain what seem to be parallels between the Duke's doings and some of the bloodier moments in the Bible. Whether such parallels were intended or not, they add an extra dimension to Bruegel's beautiful pictures.

In this detail from Bruegel's *Massacre of the Innocents,* a somber, bearded figure in black impassively watches his swordsmen and lancers butcher baby boys as their unarmed parents weep, struggle or turn away sickened. Various scholars have speculated that the black-clad horseman is the Spanish Duke of Alba and that Bruegel intended the picture as a veiled attack on Spanish cruelty in the Netherlands. Others hold that the picture was painted before Alba's arrival in Flanders and that, therefore, no such parallel could have been intended.

*Massacre of the Innocents
(detail),* 1566-1567

The Numbering at Bethlehem, 1566

Two Biblical scenes, set in snow-covered 16th Century villages, draw the eye and the imagination into a world where homely details, Scriptural lore and historical speculation mingle. The New Testament story of King Herod's attempt to snuff out the life of the newborn Christ by murdering all boys under two years of age was familiar to Bruegel's contemporaries and had long been a popular subject for artists. But Bruegel has turned the scene *(above right)* into a marauding raid on an isolated hamlet in

Flanders. The Scriptural source for his *Numbering at Bethlehem (above)* was also well known, but Bruegel was one of the few artists ever to picture it. This was the time when Joseph—accompanied by Mary, heavy with child— traveled to Bethlehem so that he could register in the census for tax collection. Bruegel's *Bethlehem* is dominated by the cold glow of a winter sun, the jagged outline of a step-gabled house, children skating and throwing snowballs. Two great wheeled casks are drawn up before

Massacre of the Innocents, 1566–1567

the inn where the registration takes place; a pig is being butchered for a feast, chickens peck vainly at the snow. Barely discernible are Mary and Joseph, who can be recognized only by the carpenter's saw Joseph carries and the fact that Mary rides a donkey beside an ox—the two traditional animals of the Nativity. Bruegel's moral message here may be that the indifference shown to the Holy Family in Bethlehem was no less cruel than man's indifference to his neighbors in the present. Bruegel's

intent may also have been at least partly political. Toward the end of his life, his country, like Palestine at the time of Christ's birth, was ruled by a foreign dictator. Under Caesar's orders, Rome's officials had levied taxes and suppressed opposition just as Spain's emissaries collected revenues and executed rebellious Flemings in Bruegel's day. Speculations of this sort are difficult to resist. As the next pages show, they do not stop with moral messages or the historic parallels between Rome and Spain.

103

The Conversion of St. Paul, 156

In 1567, the same year that the Duke of Alba led his avenging army into the Low Countries, Bruegel painted the *Conversion of St. Paul.* Unable to proceed through hostile France, Alba was forced to sail to Italy and then march through the Alps. The picture echoes this event in a remarkable way. Although the Scriptures locate Saul, an arrogant persecutor of Christians, on the road to Damascus, Bruegel places him in the midst of a Renaissance army high in a craggy alpine setting. True to the Biblical story, Saul is lying on the ground, where he has been thrown from his horse by a blinding ray of divine light.

This is the moment of his conversion from the Jewish Saul to the Christian St. Paul. But on a nearby hill *(detail opposite)* is a large horseman clad in black and riding a white stallion, a figure strikingly similar to the one in *Massacre of the Innocents.* Whether or not this is Alba and Bruegel's picture has political overtones, it has still another, simpler, meaning. The painting can be read as an illustration of the moral adage, "Pride goeth before a fall." Doubly rich, Bruegel's picture is also a triumph of pure painting, from the splendid yellow horseman in the foreground to the distant view of sea.

During the convulsive years of religious turmoil before 1567, Calvinist sympathizers, forbidden to meet in cities, gathered in the countryside to hear "hedge sermons." Bruegel's painting of John the Baptist preaching outside Jerusalem seems to portray just such an assembly. To further the parallel, St. John—shown wearing a brown tunic and pointing to the blue-robed Christ—was put to death, as were many Calvinists, for preaching heresy, in St. John's case Christianity. Bruegel's crowd, moreover, is a motley group that might have flocked out of a polyglot

The Sermon of St. John the Baptist, 1566

trading center like Antwerp—peasants, craftsmen, members of the gentry, a tall figure in an Oriental pigtail, even Catholic monks and nuns. In the large crowd a few highly individualized faces can be seen—the man peering from behind a tree at left, the members of the stately group in the trees at the extreme right and, most provocative because he is so centrally located, the man in the beret having his fortune told. Bruegel may have expected his viewers to know these people and to draw some special conclusion from their presence at an outlawed meeting.

107

The Carrying of the Cross, 1564

Bruegel's miraculous skill at blending everyday life with Biblical drama is brilliantly illustrated by *The Carrying of the Cross*. The picture swarms with activity and with people—more than 500 have been counted—a torrent of Flemish humanity that almost engulfs Christ as He labors beneath His Cross in the middle distance. The setting is clearly Calvary hill, but it could be just outside 16th Century Antwerp. The scenery, however, includes such incongruous features as a preposterous rocky

outcropping with a windmill (a device borrowed from earlier "cosmic landscape" painters) and a hazy, distant dome, perhaps to suggest the Church of the Holy Sepulchre in Jerusalem. One of the most engrossing qualities of Bruegel's complex compositions is that they can be broken down into smaller pictures, each one to be savored for its own sake. The detail opposite shows, in the shadow of a tall torture wheel, the crowd rushing toward the distant crosses eager for the proceedings to begin.

Even when seen close-up, as in this central detail, *The Carrying of the Cross,* like many of Bruegel's paintings, is full of more incidental human activity than the eye can easily follow. Along the top at the right, a man stoops to retrieve his lost cap; at the left, two small children stand as if bemused by the commotion. In the lower right corner, a girl daintily hikes up her skirt as she wades a puddle and gestures for help to a boy who has already crossed.

Sweeping from left to right is the central action, a cavalcade of cruelty and motion, based on the Bible but

pulsing with contemporary life. Bruegel pictured Christ fallen beneath the weight of the Cross, and included a cart bearing the two thieves who were to be crucified with Him. Mud drips from the turning cartwheels reflected in the shuddering water. A triumphant banner is unfurled.

The throngs of excited Flemings who press forward are pictured as no better or worse than the rest of mankind. They are not crucifying Christ. They are merely out to enjoy one of man's persistently popular forms of public entertainment—a good outdoor execution.

II2

V

Low Life in High Art

Bruegel's three most characteristic subjects are combined in this one painting—landscape, peasants and proverbs. In this case the proverb is a Flemish version of "a bird in the hand . . ." that reads, "He who knows where the nest is has the knowledge, he who robs it has the nest." The powerful peasant shown pointing to the boy rifling the bird's nest has the bland expression and the bulky, tubular legs peculiar to Bruegel's ungraceful but convincing treatment of the human body.

The Peasant and the Birdnester, 1568

Well along in his life, probably about 1567 when his creative powers were at their mellowest, Pieter Bruegel painted a peaceful and unassuming picture called *Peasant Wedding (pages 134-135).* The setting, naturally, is rural—a marriage feast taking place inside a Flemish barn. Stout guests are ranged on benches along both sides of a big trestle table backed by a wall of closely stacked hay. In the foreground two beefy men carry a door pressed into service as a huge tray laden with what looks like some sort of mush. At the left a young man is hospitably pouring beer into the first of a pile of earthenware jugs. Beside him a small girl wearing a floppy, grown-up hat skewered with a large peacock feather greedily eats mush with her hands.

To look at this picture is almost as good as being invited to the wedding itself. For although the scene is general, the various members of the wedding party are seen closely enough to be portrayed in detail as individuals. Anyone studying the picture for long begins to wonder, as he might at a real wedding reception, just who these people are and what role they played in the recent ceremony. The bride is easy enough to locate—a plump farmer's daughter smugly ensconced under a makeshift tapestry and paper crown hung incongruously from a pitchfork thrust handle-first into the hay. But where, among this jovial company, are the bride's parents? And the bridegroom's? And just which lucky fellow is the new husband?

Bruegel fanciers and art critics have often amused themselves trying to answer these questions. Their tentative conclusions are all based on the concrete evidence to be found in the rich store of realistic detail provided by the painter: how the guests are seated at table, the kinds of clothes they wear, even family resemblances of face and figure. Bruegel composed these elements in an unpretentious style. There is nothing contrived looking about the scene. Art has concealed art so successfully that the guests seem to be going about their eating and drinking just as if they had been caught unawares by a modern candid photographer working unnoticed with a small, fast camera.

Indeed, the painting looks so entirely natural, and we are today so ac-

Bruegel's *Children's Games,* a delightfully crowded compendium of activities, shows that the ways in which youngsters amuse themselves have changed very little in the 400-odd years since the picture was painted. The details below and on the opposite page—in which Bruegel's children often look like serious miniature adults —describe some games that are still played today.

Walking on stilts

Whipping tops

Shooting marbles

Dueling on piggyback

Leapfrogging

customed to seeing commonplace carryings-on recorded in both painting and photography, that it is hard for a present-day audience to realize how significant a picture *Peasant Wedding* is—one of the pioneering peaks of Bruegel's creative lifetime, and one of the landmarks in the history of realism as well. Few artists of the 16th Century were interested in the life of the common man as a subject for its own sake. Bruegel was one of these few—and by far the greatest. *Peasant Wedding,* except for a handful of other, less admired pictures about marriage festivities and village dances done at about the same time, is the most straightforward and natural rendering of everyday life painted in the 16th Century.

Flemish artists throughout the 15th and 16th Centuries, it is true, had exhibited a delightful and growing weakness for the painting of realistic details, and Bruegel's art stemmed from that tradition. But the inventory of objects and commonplace scenes that appeared in the paintings of these men—the slippers, firescreens and those lovely side glimpses of Flemish towns and countryside, which began with the religious paintings of Van Eyck and the Master of Flémalle—these were incidental to the principal subject of the paintings in which they appeared. The orange on the window sill in Van Eyck's marriage portrait of Giovanni Arnolfini and his bride *(pages 32-33)* is not only an orange proper but also (like the more familiar apple today) a symbol of man's state of innocence before the Fall. The Master of Flémalle's wickerwork firescreen *(page 30)* serves first as a halo for the seated Virgin and second as a firescreen. The very real looking wooden mousetrap that the same painter shows in the *Merode Altarpiece* is not merely a bit of slice-of-life realism but a literally rendered symbol of Jesus Christ, who was characterized by St. Augustine as a mousetrap made by God to entrap the devil.

However realistic their details, the intent of most Flemish paintings in the 15th and 16th Centuries was not primarily to record everyday life, but to convey piety or preachment—or to enhance the images of great princes and rich burghers. Long after the 16th Century, in fact, painting custom still had little use for what was to become the philosophy of artistic realism—that is, the belief and practice that low life is a fitting subject for high art.

For Bruegel and his age the term realism did not even exist in the sense that it is now used in art. Indeed, it was not until the 19th Century in France, with painters of proletarian subjects like Gustave Courbet, that the word "realism" was used to reflect an urge to assert the value of portraying the common man just as he is; the egalitarian political and social overtones that realism acquired there still persist today. Yet some of the aspects of latter-day realistic art—the color of low life and the vitality of the common man—obviously fascinated Bruegel, and he constantly sought ways of incorporating them into his art.

Even at the peak of his career, however, when he was painting the common man more or less directly, Bruegel still felt the need to make some didactic or symbolic comment. Straightforward as *Peasant Wedding* is, it nevertheless bears sharp traces of the moralistic painting tradition. The peacock feather in the small girl's hat, for example, was a clear warning to Bruegel's viewers about the sin of vanity. The heavy drinking in progress—underlined by the great stack of beer jugs in the foreground —harks back to traditional pictorial attacks on the practice of gluttony. Bruegel never broke with tradition. He was not a revolutionary but a pioneer, pushing further and more successfully than any of his contemporaries past the frontiers of pious realism in painting. In the process, he managed to twist many traditional Flemish painting subjects out of shape, stuffing them to overflowing with disorderly life. In fact, it sometimes seems in the work done toward the end of his career that all that remains of a traditional subject when Bruegel has finished with it is the official title.

Bruegel's painting lifetime does not break down into distinct periods by subject matter. His tendency toward realism is not characteristic of any one particular phase of his professional life either, but is a persistent inclination of eye and hand. It is discernible in everything he touched, inextricably mixed in one proportion or another with nearly every painting he undertook. This preoccupation with the world he lived in takes on several different aspects in Bruegel's work. The first, most effectively illustrated in *Peasant Wedding,* is a concern for the real men and women around him and how they behaved. Another, as we shall see, is his special kind of truthfulness in handling landscape, which he carried further than any of his contemporaries. Last, and perhaps most entertaining for modern viewers, is Bruegel's obvious fascination with how everyday things looked and worked. This lifetime interest resulted in a steadily fattening pictorial encyclopedia of details whose title might be "How Things Were Done in Flanders."

The most direct example of the latter is the picture *Children's Games,* which, as its title implies, is a catalog of scores of juvenile amusements from knucklebones to blindman's buff. But the illustrated details for Bruegel's low life encyclopedia also turn up as incidentals in many other pictures about other subjects. The list embraces everything from three-legged chairs to gallows to cooking omelettes; it includes all the tools and techniques of cutting stone and lifting loads by treadmill pulleys shown in the *Tower of Babel (pages 9-12),* the techniques of willow trimming, haymaking and pig butchering from the landscape pictures, and a kaleidoscopic view of human horseplay in *The Battle between Carnival and Lent (pages 130-131).*

This latter picture is itself a treasure house of homely details, a pageant of toys and trinkets, nuns and beggars, costumes and customs, storefronts and strolling players that could properly serve as reference material for a modern film director bent on producing a movie set in the 16th Century Netherlands. It centers around an outrageously fat-cheeked figure, decked out to stand for the Mardi Gras delights of self-indulgence, confronted by a comic, blue-jawed, knife-faced opponent, the embodiment of overzealous piety. Not only are all the backdrops accurate; so are dozens of human poses and actions, for Bruegel is one of the great masters of action in art. Like a good sports photographer, he catches his human figures at the precise instant in a jump or gesture when they look least posed and most active.

Authentic as it is in many ways, *Carnival and Lent* also illustrates one of

Guessing which hand

Riding, drumming, making mudpies

Standing on one's head

Swinging on a rail

Playing dice or jacks

the aspects in which many of Bruegel's pictures are quite intentionally inaccurate. Like the two Mardi Gras combatants, the people in this painting are not portrayed as individuals. They are, instead, drawn either as outrageous personifications of a specific human quality, like greed or fear, or as interchangeably bland, muffin-faced nonentities, abstractions of human empty-headedness—not men, but man seen in the mass.

Bruegel's figures seem closest to caricatures when he is making fun of human behavior in satiric works like *Carnival and Lent,* or in religious paintings like *The Carrying of the Cross* where the callous grossness of human nature is part of the theme. Yet it is worth noting that sometimes what now seems like extreme exaggeration to us may have been a fair enough rendering of the painter's fellow man. In Bruegel's time the common man, pressed down by ignorance, superstition, grinding work, and poverty, released from persistent anxiety only through bouts of drinking and brawling, was a brutish fellow under the best of circumstances. It is sometimes hard to decide, when Bruegel observes such people, whether he does so with a caricaturist's distorted squint or a realist's honest eye for unpleasant truth.

Bruegel never entirely abandoned caricature. But increasingly in his later years he moved closer to his subjects and included fewer and fewer people in his pictures. As he did so, he increased the amount of both realistic detail and human individuality expressed in the faces of his men and women. In shifting his characteristic composition from multitudes to a few large figures, Bruegel was borrowing from the Italian painters of his time. Such borrowing was fashionable, but most Flemish painters who did so also adopted idealized Italian styles and subjects along with the composition—massively heroic Biblical scenes full of muscular people who, as John Ruskin observed of Raphael's studies of the Disciples, "clearly could never have existed on earth or in heaven." Bruegel showed, instead, that Italian techniques could be put to the service of capturing in oils the real Flemish world, of exploring the rough, homely details of everyday living. *Peasant Wedding* is the most triumphant example—a blend of Southern skill at placing figures harmoniously so as to draw the eye of the viewer into the picture with the Northern fondness for low life lovingly detailed.

More than any other man, Bruegel, with pictures like *Peasant Wedding,* probably deserves credit for creating an art form that now goes under the name of genre realism—the straightforward depiction of simple scenes of daily life. Such scenes became extremely popular in 17th Century Holland in the paintings of Pieter de Hoogh, Jan Steen, Adrian van Ostade and many others, but, even in his own time, Bruegel was not entirely alone in his experiments in realism. In the 1540s an Amsterdam-born painter named Pieter Aertsen, working in Antwerp, became well known for showing Dutch and Flemish housewives surrounded by their families in warm kitchens. Aertsen's son-in-law, Joachim Beuckelaer, another Antwerper, who died only a few years after Bruegel, made a career as a specialist in market scenes filled with meat, vegetables and fish and crowded with townsfolk. The successful Italianate painter Frans Floris also proved his versatility from time to time by briefly abandoning his

The Painter and the Connoisseur, a pen-and-ink drawing by Bruegel, contrasts the ruggedness and intense absorption of the creative artist with the bland-featured, gawking admiration of the potential purchaser. Bruegel pokes some fun at the collector by showing that he needs glasses to see well and by catching him in the act of fingering money in his purse. Whether he is about to pay the artist or is suspiciously checking on his cash is left for the viewer to decide. Artists of the 16th and 17th Centuries admired this drawing so much that it is one of Bruegel's most copied works.

classical subject matter to situate a Holy Family cosily in a *gemütlich* Flemish interior.

Common subjects, however, tended for one reason or another to be of only occasional interest to these men. Floris' true bent was toward the Italian Renaissance. Beuckelaer could not find patrons and had to give up his work to make a living filling in costume details in the portraits done by Antonio Moro. Aertsen was the best of the three, yet his common folk somehow suggest refined romantic models posing in rustic dress. It was left to Bruegel to create a body of work that stands as the most complete pictorial record of the everyday world that his century produced.

That 16th Century Flemish world, as revealed in Pieter Bruegel's paintings, has two rather startling aspects: the enormous amount of carousing that goes on and the prevalence of cripples. Even after allowing for artistic license, one is inclined to wonder whether there could actually have been so much of both. The answer seems to be yes. Contemporary records for the 16th Century are sparse, but clearly it is not entirely by chance that the legendary inventor of beer is a Fleming, a quasi-mythical King of Beer named Gambrinus, who obviously had the best and most notorious interest of his countrymen at heart. An Italian visitor in Flanders at the time noted that the people of the Netherlands would gladly walk 40 miles to go to a drinking party, and many other contemporary references confirm the conclusion that Flemings, like Germans, were famous for tipsy brawling. That weakness was matched by a proclivity for dancing, singing and rough-and-tumble horseplay—all practiced at a yearly succession of fetes, saint's days and fairs that must have taxed everyone's capacity for desperate merriment.

For the gregarious Flemings, even private parties became a kind of public institution. Most neighbors and all relatives, no matter how distant, had to be invited to birthdays and weddings. Individual families still observed the medieval autumnal festival of the butchery, when animals, which were to supply meat for the winter, were butchered and dressed down in the street. *La boucherie* usually escalated into a party that often involved an entire quarter of the town. Bonfires were built. Parts of the steer were cooked and eaten—for many of the poorest guests this was the only meat they got all year. And anyone glutted with roast could try another specialty, omelettes dished up with plenty of lard—like the one being cooked outdoors by the old woman in Bruegel's *Carnival and Lent.*

Saint's days dotted the calendar—each one with its characteristic festivity. The best was November 11, St. Martin's Day. To honor the patron saint of innkeepers, Flemings built bonfires, knocked on strange doors as a joke, ate tiny pancakes and roast duck and, habitually, drank themselves stupid. All this naturally appealed to Pieter Bruegel. A fragment remains of a very large St. Martin's Day painting he did, and a 17th Century engraving exists that was based on a Bruegel composition showing an uproarious crowd of tipplers scrimmaging around a wine barrel approximately as big as Noah's ark. Bruegel may have done other versions of the theme, too, because Pieter Bruegel the Younger honored St. Martin in several pictures—and the son often copied his illustrious father.

The show of shows, when it came to public festivities, was the *kermesse.* Begun as a glorified church fair (from *kerke messe),* the *kermesse* gradually evolved into a twice-a-year gathering of villagers from a given region who plunged into an orgy of buying and selling, drinking and yelling— a communal explosion of joy marked by what a French historian has described, with apparent accuracy, as *passions grossières.* Tents and trestle tables filled the streets of the chosen village site. The trade guilds paraded. Wares were displayed. An ox was cooked and eaten. During the celebration—it could last as long as two weeks—dancing and singing seldom stopped; bawdy plays like "The Ugly Bride" in *Carnival and Lent* were performed; bakers distributed a kind of sugar cookie, suggestively called an "all for love."

One favorite prank was to stop strangers and douse them with beer followed by fistfuls of flour or gobbets of hot wax. To prove the efficiency of their product, rat poison salesmen swung strings of their victims in the air. Showmen exhibited madwomen gibbering in their chains. Young folk joined hands to skate barefoot on hard ground made slippery with ripe garbage. Organized fights pitted blind men armed with clubs against each other, as well as stout peasants armed with specially blunted knives to permit the maximum amount of bloodletting with the minimum amount of manslaughter. Half the spectator sport, however, was provided by the impromptu fights that broke out continually as burly Flemings, marinated for days in beer or wine, suddenly let fly at one another. For beneath the frantic surface jollity lay somber violence. Behind that, as Bruegel's pictures often show, lay poverty, superstition, sickness and fear of death.

As a caricaturist Bruegel best summed up the persistently stark contrasts of his world in the swarming activities of *The Battle between Carnival and Lent.* Here beggars mix with party-goers blithely costumed as kings; rioters caper briskly cheek by jowl with cripples who can barely get about on hand crutches and the callused nubs of what once were knees. In these portrayals, as elsewhere, Bruegel has made no appeal for sympathy—most of them are ugly creatures armed like cornered bats with only teeth-gnashing rage against the world; in picturing the gnarled ugliness of the cripples he has provided an unforgettable portrait of deformity.

The artist accomplished something subtler and more rare in a picture like *The Peasant Dance (pages 136-139),* where the exaggeration of caricature is much less pronounced. Here he has moved in close on the faces of people—such as the irascibly intent bagpiper and the drunken confidant next to him—and has skillfully managed to give us a glimpse of the underlying anger and sadness that shadow their attempts to have a howling good time.

In Bruegel's world, as in the Middle Ages, the precarious balance between life and death is always felt, captured perhaps in the portrayal of the moments of cheer that relieve a lifetime of numbing work and poverty. The awareness comes as more of a surprise in connection with the 16th Century than with the Middle Ages, though, because historians have led us to think of Bruegel's age as the morning of modern times, when great advances in learning, science and exploration occurred. Unhappily, despite the accomplishments of men like Magellan and Copernicus, Gutenberg and Erasmus, mankind in general lived exactly as it had for centuries—and would for centuries to come.

Nowhere is the lag between scientific breakthrough and change in the daily human condition more sharply illustrated than in the field of medicine. One of Bruegel's contemporaries, the unschooled French genius Ambroise Paré, became the principal pioneer of modern surgical techniques. Paré worked as a doctor first with the busy armies of Francis I and was physician to the next four French kings: Henry II, Francis II, Charles IX and Henry III. He devised new ways for successfully amputating limbs, taking stitches in flesh without leaving a hideous scar and controlling loss of blood during operations. Bruegel's fellow Brussels townsman, Andreas Vesalius, by 1543 had laid the groundwork for modern anatomy, disproving in the process much of the hodgepodge of misinformation that had served as medical gospel since the Third Century, when it was expounded by the Greek physician, Galen.

The Low Countries, in fact, were correctly regarded as being highly advanced in medicine. Yet most surgeons were still no more than barbers equipped with straight razors and an excess of zeal. As a remedy for fever, doctors were still regularly prescribing spider heads hung around the neck in clamshells. People firmly believed they could cure a bloody nose by letting a few drops of blood fall from it onto a red-hot iron. What the medical standards of 16th Century Flanders meant in common practice was that nearly everyone who came down with any of the many ills, which today are treated and cured as a matter of course, would either die or end up in some way marked for life.

Especially among the poor and rural folk, broken legs, arms, wrists and ankles were seldom treated. Very few people knew how. A clean break might heal only slightly bent. Compound fractures were hopeless, for they usually led either to gangrene or a limb healed in some strange, unusable shape. For the few victims fortunate enough to survive an amputation, performed most probably by a barber without benefit of antiseptic or anesthetic, there was the prospect of a life spent hobbling about on a stump or on some of the ingenious leg and arms crutches that the age devised. The appallingly twisted creatures shown by Bruegel in so many of his paintings are not nightmarish exaggerations—in one sense they are lucky survivors.

Just how accurate Bruegel's portrayal was of the cripples and their crutches has been verified in a most unusual way. In 1958 Anthony Torrilhon, a young French physician with an ingenious turn of mind, submitted the various illnesses depicted in Bruegel's pictures to modern methods of diagnosis. He published a doctoral thesis that concludes flatly that to portray so many human ills with such clinical accuracy Pieter Bruegel must have been trained as a physician.

Dr. Torrilhon maintains, and amply documents his findings, that Bruegel painted the sick and the halt and the lame of his time with such pitiless clarity that in many cases a modern doctor can have a reasonable chance of diagnosing what was wrong with them. The afflictions of Brue-

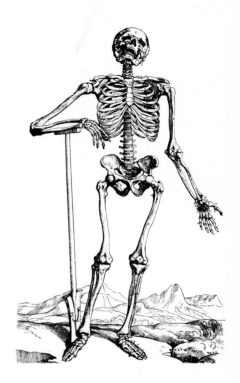

A gesturing skeleton posed as a gravedigger and a flayed man standing in an Italian landscape are among the instructive woodcuts of the human body from Andreas Vesalius' monumental treatise on anatomy, published in 1543 and illustrated by artists in the workshop of the Venetian master Titian. Vesalius, a Flemish contemporary of Bruegel, was a pioneer anatomist, and his book was one of the first great works of modern science. Born in Brussels, Vesalius spent much of his life in Italy, and was for a time a court physician to Philip II of Spain.

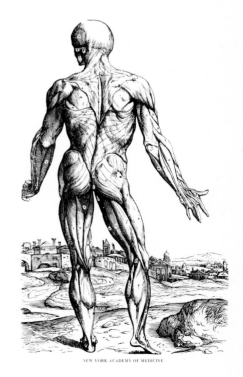

In Bruegel's *The Blind Leading the Blind,* a chain of blind men linked to each other by outstretched hands and wooden staves, inexorably follow their leader toward a headlong tumble into a meandering brook. Based on Christ's words, "If the blind lead the blind, both shall fall into the ditch," the picture is a remarkable example of the accuracy of Bruegel's eye and hand—for the victims suffer from observably different diseases of the eye, and their various positions from left to right mark a dynamic progression from erect balance to flat-out fall, like the successive collapse of a row of dominoes. The picture was painted in 1568 when Bruegel was living in Brussels, and citizens of the Belgian capital now believe that the painter's models for the background chapel, house and stream were found in the tiny suburban village of Pede St. Anne where similar buildings and scenery still exist.

gel's many cripples, according to Torrilhon, are varied and identifiable. They range from spasmodic paraplegia—illustrated by the central cripple with bells on his boots in *The Cripples (pages 132-133)*—to advanced locomotor ataxia—an outgrowth of syphilis—and include maladies that waste and curl the legs and result in only four toes on each foot, the condition of some of the cripples shown in *Carnival and Lent.*

Equally accurate, apparently, are the various kinds of orthopedic aids that Bruegel depicted. They correspond exactly to objects surviving in medical histories and museums: rough, t-shaped crutches; miniature wooden sawhorses used by men with strong torsos but wasted legs to pull themselves along; a special kind of flat pan on which 16th Century cripples used to slither over the ground more easily; special wooden platforms strapped below the knees to act as shoes for people who had lost their feet; and even wooden shin guards worn by some blind men to protect them from coming up painfully against the sharp edges of their darkened world.

Pictures of the blind are, according to Dr. Torrilhon, the *pièce de résistance* of Bruegel's medical observation. *The Blind Leading the Blind,* a picture painted in 1568, just a year before Bruegel died, presents five lurching figures, each one blindly following the one ahead of him, and a sixth who has already fallen in a brook. Among them, clinically observed and recorded, says Torrilhon, are five separate kinds of blindness. One man, for instance, has a white filmy growth over his cornea, which can have resulted only from a disease now known as leucoma. Another figure, staring blankly up toward the sky, suffers from atrophy of the eyeball resulting from damage to the optic nerve by permanently neglected glaucoma. As a modern doctor, Torrilhon is more impressed by Bruegel's acute perception of blindness than of other ills because, in the 16th Century, so little was known about it. Flemish doctors in Bruegel's lifetime customarily ascribed eye trouble to toxic vapor that rose from the patient's stomach and leaked into the brain. Their counsel to eye strain sufferers was: "Have someone blow in the eye gently with a breath sweetened by chewing cloves or fennel."

Dr. Torrilhon's theory about Bruegel's medical training cannot be proved or disproved by the known facts of his life, but the doctor's knowledgeable detective work clearly proves Bruegel's uncanny skill as an observer and painter. In *The Blind Leading the Blind* these qualities are all the more remarkable because the subject is not primarily realistic but didactic. *The Blind Leading the Blind* was a stock, moralizing subject painted to illustrate a Biblical proverb from Matthew XV: "Let them alone. They are blind guides. And if the blind lead the blind, both shall fall into the ditch." Hieronymus Bosch in painting the subject used only the two blind men stipulated by the Biblical lines. Bruegel not only increased the number to six to give himself a horizontal composition; he also went far beyond the conventional boundaries of realism. That he saw fit to use such naturalistic accuracy in painting the faces and eyes of his symbolic blind men is an example of his persistent attempts to spice traditional art form with lifelike details.

Bruegel's way of treating a didactic theme represents a culmination of the Flemish tradition, begun by Van Eyck and the Master of Flémalle, of lending convincing authenticity to symbolism by using familiar objects as symbols. Van Eyck's symbolic orange looks real enough to eat. The symbolic mousetrap in the Master of Flémalle's *Merode Altarpiece* would really catch a mouse—as well as its intended symbolic prey, the devil. Bruegel's blind men, symbols of the blindness of mankind in pursuing worldly aims despite the knowledge of Christ's teachings, are not handled artistically as stock figures of blindness. They suffer precisely from glaucoma.

One of Carel van Mander's more intriguing stories about Pieter Bruegel is his assertion that the painter used to dress up in rustic garb, go out into the country and crash peasant parties in order to collect local color for his paintings. Van Mander's anecdote and the unerring accuracy of Bruegel's details both suggest that he may have produced stacks of quick sketches, first dashed off in the fields and streets and then worked up into oil paintings at leisure in the studio.

Bruegel did, in fact, leave about 40 ink-over-chalk sketches *(pages 125-128)* showing human figures, as well as a few horses, a stag and a solitary bison. He even carefully labeled each one with a variation of the phrase *naer het leven,* Dutch for "from the life." With characteristic concern for detail he also jotted down the colors that should be used in transposing them to oil paintings. The confusing point is that only two of these sketches ever turn up in any of Bruegel's surviving paintings—a study of a monk and a barely discernible pair of spectators in the middle distance, both in *The Carrying of the Cross.* Apparently no other figures—of all the hundreds and hundreds that exist in the paintings—came directly from any of the surviving *naer het leven* sketches.

Conceivably this could be explained by the fact that many paintings and drawings have been lost. Bruegel no doubt left hundreds of drawings to his sons, who may possibly have used and re-used them in their own painting until the original sketches crumbled away. But even so, pure chance would make it unlikely that the only *naer het leven* drawings to survive would be the ones *not* used as source material for Bruegel's surviving paintings.

Another, perhaps more significant explanation lies in the nature of the *naer het leven* drawings themselves. At first glance they seem to resemble lifelike sketches by a number of old masters, sure of hand and sharp of line. A few actually do have the same quality as old master drawings, and in these few the deftly caught slump of a tired peasant body and the wizened tracery of a face speak to us in compelling shorthand of lives lived out in poverty some four centuries ago. Among them are two old Jews in fur hats huddling together over a Talmudic text, a sleeping washerwoman's weathered face settling into the weary folds of her voluminous clothing, a country woman swathed in sheepskin sitting at market, her arms clasped to her for warmth, obviously perishing of cold as she waits for someone to buy the few mean vegetables she has spread before her on an upside-down basket.

But a closer look at the drawing shows that these few are exceptions. The rest of the *naer het leven* are "from the life" only in a very special sense. In most of them Bruegel avoids the difficult job of trying to catch a swift individual likeness in face or pose. He sometimes does as many as three studies of the same figure without ever showing the face. Customarily he presents people from the back or squashes a hat down on the head so far that the face is entirely hidden. When he sketches a farmer riding home on one of a pair of plowhorses, the man's clothes, the bit and bridle, all the rig of the horses are done in loving detail. But the farmer's face is turned away. Bruegel certainly sketched these things from life, but what he wanted was not life but details of dress. The pictures are studded with belts and scabbards, pouches and crutches and shepherd's crooks, nearly a dozen different kinds of headgear, shawls and mufflers and leather boots (in an age when leather boots were a rare and prized possession).

What the *naer het leven* drawings most resemble are quick penciled notes by a fashion designer or by someone roughing out costumes for the theater, both of them concentrating on what the fashion world calls accessories—shoes, belts, gloves, hats. If Bruegel used the sketches in his painting it was certainly not as direct raw material for finished figures but only to refresh his memory about what kinds of equipment the people in his paintings should wear.

Just as Bruegel seems to have made most sparing use of his *naer het leven* sketches, he also seems to have skipped certain preliminary compositional steps normally taken by artists of his time. They customarily worked up paintings in their studios, not only from sketches from nature, but also from live models and from groupings of figures observed in the works of other artists. The whole pattern was laboriously roughed out in charcoal on paper before anything, even an outline, was put on the final wooden painting surface. But no preparatory sketches of this type by Bruegel exist.

That the man who painted the real world in more detail and at greater length than anyone in his century may have done so without these cus-

Artists' studios during Bruegel's time often served as schools and were frequently crowded with young students, models and assistants like the ones shown in this contemporary engraving. At center, a master artist works on a large painting of St. George and the Dragon. The two young apprentices nearby blend his colors, while assistants behind him grind fresh pigments. Another student in the left foreground copies a classical bust, and behind him a workshop artist paints a portrait.

tomary aids to composition suggests that Bruegel must have possessed a visual memory of a precision and intensity that was remarkable even among artists, who usually have a great capacity for retaining images. It also suggests that he had an imagination so powerful that he could assemble vast, teeming scenes in his head bit by bit and then, holding all the compositional elements frozen in some corner of his mind, paint from that mental image directly upon wood. To get a small idea of how difficult such a thing would be, look at any of his busy pictures—*The Carrying of the Cross,* for instance *(pages 108-111)*—and then, shutting your eyes, try to remember even for a few seconds the arrangement of just a few details.

Bruegel's powers of interior reflection offer a partial explanation of why realistic paintings of simple scenes like *Peasant Wedding* are also monumental works of art—while similar pictures executed by the 17th Century genre painters who followed are little more than anecdotes. David Teniers II, for instance, often shows us accurately enough how a few old codgers played at bowls on a dusty village street. Adriaen van Ostade opens the door on a handful of fat men smoking and drinking themselves to sleep in a shadowy inn. Such scenes offer momentary pleasure and then are quickly forgotten.

Bruegel's portraits of life are not so easily displaced. The world he painted was at the same time a representative part of 16th Century Flanders and a private province of his mind. His pictures linger in our memory because they are the products not only of sharp observation but also of a creative imagination that has had time to brood upon reality and transform it. Pieter Bruegel's Flanders is both real and imaginary, a personal creation whose nearest parallel lies not in art but in 20th Century literature—William Faulkner's Yoknapatawpha County, a complete world, which both is and is not part of the state of Mississippi. Flemish painting's outstanding realist, seen in this light, was neither a color cameraman nor a cheerful reporter. He was a pictorial novelist.

"From the Life"

Born in the country, Pieter Bruegel knew the life of the common people of Flanders intimately. And although he spent most of his time in cities—the only place he could pursue his career—he made frequent forays to nearby villages, recording with obvious delight their boisterous, rough-handed way of life. In quick sketches like the ones opposite, which he called *naer het leven* (from the life), he stored up details for use in future paintings. Later, in his studio, Bruegel combined these images with his vivid memories and created scenes of villagers cavorting in squares at carnival time, and dancing and drinking at feasts and weddings.

Bruegel's "peasant" pictures include farmers, rural merchants, itinerant monks and musicians as well as peasant laborers. But in an age when artists concentrated on Biblical stories and classical myths, and showed very little interest in portraying rustic life, Bruegel's down-to-earth subject matter was startling. His popularization of this straightforward approach to everyday life led to what is known as genre painting. Together with the legend of his own lowly birth, it earned him the nickname "Peasant" Bruegel from succeeding generations. But the painter seems to have been quite a sophisticated man, who in his early years probably chose homely subjects because they best suited his satirizing of human foibles. As he grew older, however, the drolleries were stripped away, and Bruegel showed the world just as it was.

Black chalk-and-ink studies from life, these sketches show two peasant women with their wares at market. One, bundled against the cold, is hunched over a basket of vegetables; the other, with what looks like a basket of hay strung over her shoulder, seems to be scrabbling at small change in her lap. The signature "H. Bosch" was perhaps added by a confused collector ignorant of Bruegel's style.

Two market women, c.1558

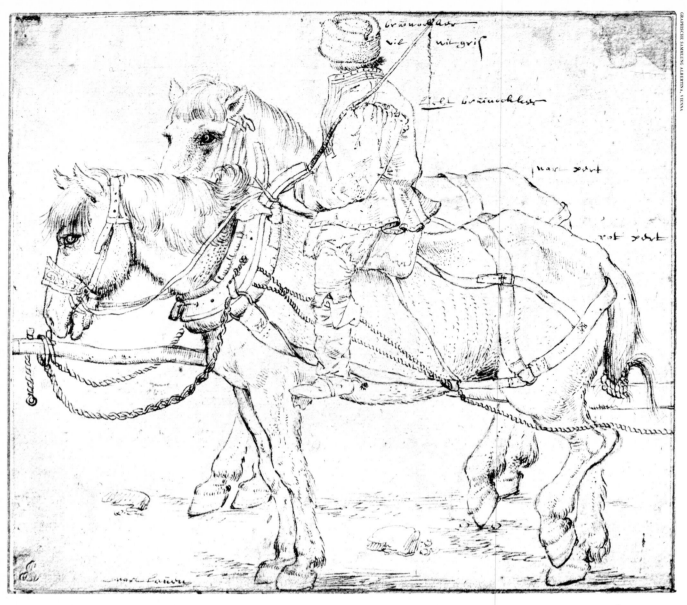

Team of horses, c.1564

At least seventy-seven of Bruegel's *naer het leven* sketches still exist, and, as the examples on these pages show, they illustrate many different kinds of people, both country and city folk. Roughly drawn on the spot in chalk and refined later, usually in brown ink, they are remarkably detailed. The wagoner above, comfortably astride one of his weary nags, sits in a tangle of harness—bits, bridles, straps and rope—all meticulously accurate. The two rabbis hunched over a huge volume of Talmudic commentary *(top right, opposite)* are properly bearded, hatted and robed. Bruegel even shows the Star of David brooch that one man wears to hold his shawl in place.

The scribbled words that appear beside the figures are Bruegel's notes on the colors of various articles of clothing and objects. That he was so careful to observe and jot down these things seems to show that the artist intended to use his drawings as a basis for paintings. Yet very few of the known drawings have a parallel in his extant oil paintings. Additionally, few of the sketches depict the faces of his subjects or the lively postures that so often characterize Bruegel's full-scale pictures. The answer to this mystery may be that Bruegel made use of the *naer het leven* material in another way, treating the sketches as a kind of dictionary of details—about things like clothing and equipment—to reinforce his memory while he was putting the finishing touches on a painting. Like other great artists who were essentially painters—Rembrandt and Rubens, for example—Bruegel may have sketched as an exercise for his hand and his eye, but when he faced his easel with a paint-laden brush, his imaginative power to invoke reality took over.

Seated peasant asleep, c.1565

Two rabbis, c.1563-1564

Three studies, on the left a cripple, on the right a soldier, after 1560

Two peasants, one in profile, the other seen from the back, after 1564

As his *naer het leven* sketches indicate, Bruegel was far more interested in characterizing human types than in portraying particular individuals. Catching an expressive posture—the slump of the shoulder of the old man above, for instance—the angle of a bent leg or the crush of a garment, he was able to describe a great deal. In the drawings he almost never shows faces. In painting he seldom isolates individuals. Even the poor old woman opposite, the only extant single head by Bruegel, is not the subject of a traditional portrait. It clearly lacks the inventory of specific facial details that make portraits so interesting. What Bruegel has done is to portray a general human condition and the particular emotion of a moment —in this case awe, fear or perhaps superstition. And he has done it so compellingly that the woman, like the people in his crowded later scenes, seems alive and real.

Head of an old peasant woman, c. 1568

Today's Mardi Gras celebrations had a counterpart in Bruegel's Flanders—a three-day festival of frantic eating, drinking and carousing that preceded the 40 days of Lent, the period of penitence when pious countrymen drank plain water, ate little but fish, played not at all. The carnival, which offered a rich display of man at his most outrageous extremes of behavior, naturally appealed to Bruegel's satiric eye. To do the festival justice, he painted one of his earliest *Wimmelbilder* (literally, a teeming people-picture). This panoramic bird's-eye view is centered on a mock battle—a traditional part of the festivities—in which the piety of Lent was comically pitted against the revelry of Carnival. At the center, a brightly dressed, grossly fat man representing Carnival's excesses is mounted on a huge beer barrel, ready to joust with Lent, a scrawny creature clad in mourning and seated on an uncomfortable prayer stool. Carnival brandishes a cooking spit garnished with rich holiday food while Lent weakly wields a baker's paddle holding two mean herring. Behind Carnival, to the left and down the side streets in the background, masked revelers wolf waffles, quaff beer and dance gaily. Before the Inn of the Blue Boat, comedians act out a broad farce called "The Ugly Bride," while a couple kisses in the window above.

In contrast with the brawling left side of the picture, where begging cripples are completely ignored, the right side is filled with piety and charity. Dark-robed worshipers stream from an austere church, a fishwife does a thriving trade beside a well and kindly burghers dispense alms.

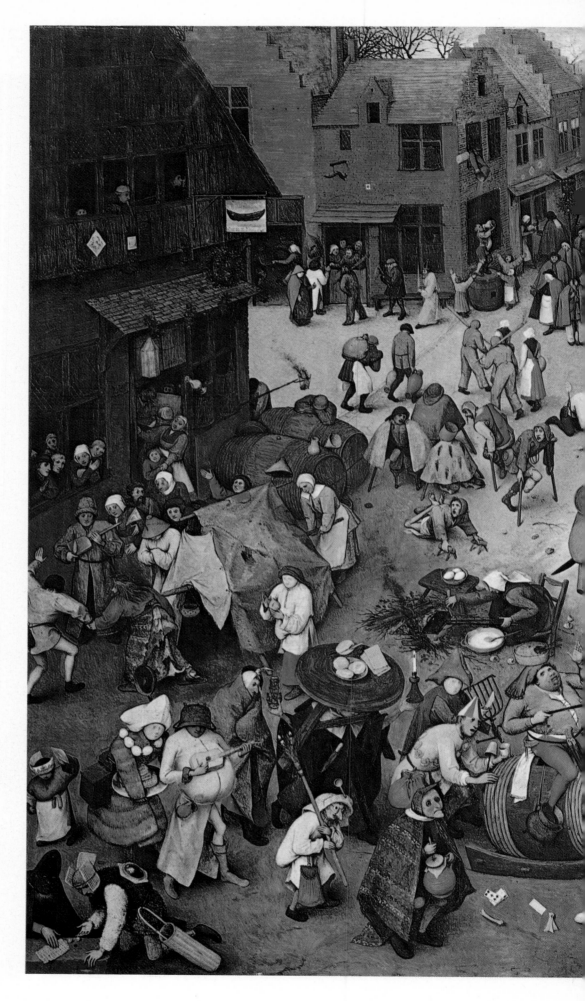

The Battle between Carnival and Lent, 1559

The Cripples, 1568

Bruegel's pictures of common people, like his religious and didactic paintings, can be read on several levels. Taken at face value, this painting seems to be merely a shockingly realistic portrayal of five miserable cripples and an old crone begging for handouts. People like these, disabled by war, by disease and by their own wracking poverty, were an everyday sight in Bruegel's Flanders. And like Bosch before him, Bruegel seems to have been fascinated by them—a group very like this one appears in *Carnival and Lent.* Nine years after he completed that painting, Bruegel returned to the subject and narrowed his focus in this small picture, which is reproduced here larger than actual size.

Beneath the surface of this painting are several levels of symbolic suggestion that can hardly have escaped Bruegel's contemporaries who saw deformed bodies as cruel proof that an erring man was paying the wages of sin through loss of the symmetry ordained by God. In addition to this harshly didactic lesson, the picture can be interpreted as an illustration of a proverb, perhaps the old Dutch maxim, "Lies go lame as if on crutches." Seen in historic context, the picture may also have sharp social and political nuances. All the hats worn by the cripples are different. Some of them, particularly the mock bishop's mitre worn by the man on the right and the soldier's red shako on the left, suggest the official headgear of members of the establishment. However, it is the subject itself that seems most provocative of multiple meaning. During the years before Bruegel painted *The Cripples* a dissident group of Flemish noblemen, agitating against Spanish dominance in the Low Countries, took the nickname "Beggars" from a haughty jeer flung at them by a Spanish sympathizer. Adopting the name quite literally, they carried beggar's bowls and wore chains and foxtails— the traditional beggar's emblem seen in the painting. In time, as popular support for their cause grew, the nobles' rebellion erupted into a full-scale war for independence against Spain, and "Long live the Beggars" became a national rallying cry.

133

Peasant Wedding, 1568

In one of his most cheerful portraits of Flemish life, Bruegel shows a party of reasonably well-to-do farmers, with a scattering of townsfolk, sitting down to a wedding feast. The setting is a barn that has been cleaned up for the occasion. The guests gather at a harvest table surrounded by rough wooden benches and stools. Clay jugs provide beer goblets; an old door functions as a serving tray. There is no mistaking the smiling bride, seated beneath a paper crown that hangs on a green cloth. But generations of viewers and critics have never quite been able to decide which is the bridegroom or who the other wedding guests might be. Probably the most convincing analysis has been offered by critic Gilbert Highet, who bases his judgments on facial similarities, place at table and differences in dress. The physical resemblance of the bride to the young man at the far left pouring beer and the man at the head of the table handing out plates suggests they are her brothers. The bride's mother may be the woman partly hidden at her right because, Highet reasons, it is the groom's parents who are seated on the bride's left— at least they occupy a place of honor, bear no resemblance to the bride and wear rich, citified clothes. Beside them sit a monk and a man whose sword and fancy tunic suggest that he is too grand a match for the bride; probably he is the party's most distinguished guest, perhaps a local burgomaster. Having eliminated all other major figures, Highet's choice as bridegroom falls on the mean-faced, long-nosed fellow leaning back from the table and raising his jug to ask for more drink. He wears city clothes, too, and resembles the couple previously identified as his parents. Whether the speculation is correct, the painting is so rich in realistic details that it invites long and careful scrutiny.

The most prolonged and riotous holiday enjoyed by the Flemish peasantry was the *kermesse*, a combined fair and fete held annually on the feast day of the local patron saint. During the celebration a whole village might be turned upside-down for a week or more while villagers (like these) danced to the tunes of traveling bagpipers, drank homebrew and bought housewares, cloth and trinkets from booths set up by itinerant merchants.

Distant ancestors of the decorous church bazaars of today, *kermesses* became so popular in Flanders that some villages took to holding two of them each year. It seems likely that a *kermesse* provided Bruegel with the subject for this picture. Though Bruegel's picture concentrates on the fringes of the crowd, away from the noisy booths, he offers a number of specific clues that indicate it is *kermesse* time: the flower-decked picture of the Virgin pinned to a tree, the jester entertaining a group at center, the gay banner floating over the door of what appears to be the local inn and the fact that the village church figures so prominently in the background.

A late work, the painting is vastly different from Bruegel's earlier crowded scenes like *Carnival and Lent.* Dancing and drinking go on apace, as before, but now Bruegel presents the people from eye level and moves up close, concentrating on a few figures—the wildly gesturing group at the trestle table; dancers stepping to the drone of a lusty piper. These men and women, as the detail on the following pages shows, are presented not as satiric caricatures but as real people, whose heavy hands, rude gestures, and weathered faces reveal the wear and tear of their daily work.

The Peasant Dance, 1568

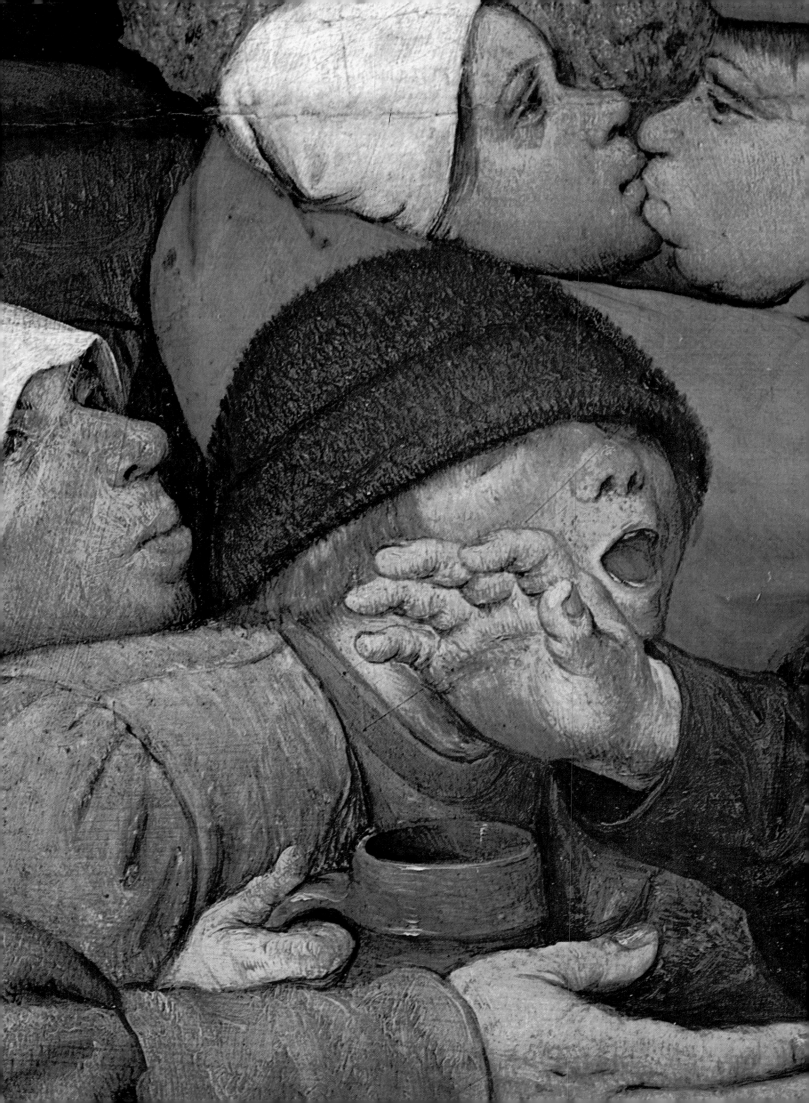

Om dat de werelt is soe ongetru
Daer om gha ic in den ru

VI

In Dispraise
of Folly

A gloomy old man wrapped in a black cloak loses his fortune to a cutpurse in one of Bruegel's last paintings. Above the Flemish caption ("Because the world is so untrue, I go my way so full of rue"), he walks a path strewn with triangular burrs called "man traps" in the Netherlands. The painting, which has been heavily retouched, suggests that the old man is partly to blame for his own misfortune. He is so absorbed in his own misanthropy that he does not notice the wily thief who wears a globe, showing that he represents the thievish nature of the world.

The Misanthrope, 1568

Tourists carrying notebooks and magnifying glasses have been known to disappear into the Bruegel room of Vienna's Kunsthistorisches Museum on a sunny morning and not emerge until late afternoon. This peculiar power of Bruegel's paintings to inspire prolonged and microscopic scrutiny is partly attributable to a specific fact of art history. In Bruegel's time painting was still enjoyed partly as a form of literature. Good pictures, like good books, were created to be pored over long and lovingly, both for amusement and for instruction. In marked contrast to many present-day painters who seem to feel no need to offer subject and substance, a 16th Century Flemish master was expected to make each oil provide viewers with a lifetime supply of worthwhile studying.

Since the improvement of man was still an important role of art, a painting had to be didactic to be considered worthwhile. To be personally absorbing as well, it had to be loaded with details that could be lingered over and enjoyably identified. But where were such familiar details to come from? The Bible, of course, was a rich source of fascinating tales and characters. Yet the Bible only went so far. Historic events and classic myths were coming into fashion as artistic themes, but more slowly in the north of Europe than in Italy. For Flemish painters seeking a "busy" subject, the solution sometimes lay in illustrated proverbs, which provided instantly recognizable and highly entertaining subject matter.

They admirably served a further didactic purpose in that they were a painter's most effective ammunition for sharpshooting at human folly. Sixteenth Century artists, like men in any age, were confronted by a rich array of man's foibles to satirize; but probably in no other country or century than in 16th Century Flanders could painters count on a public familiar with more down-to-earth proverbs that could serve both to illustrate folly and reprove it.

Today, especially in the United States, we are less preoccupied with human folly, and the practice of quoting gritty proverbs has fallen into decline. Proverbs, when we think of them at all, amount to little more than a few old wheezes about crying over spilt milk, occasional citations from the Bible ("Fear of the Lord is the beginning of wisdom") and rare, salty borrowings from countries perhaps a bit closer to their peasant past than we are, such as Nikita Khrushchev's celebrated observation that "shrimps will learn to whistle" before the Soviet Union will abandon its Marxist principles. The very word "folly" now sounds fussy and old-fashioned. At most it suggests nothing more significant than a minor fall from virtue by a genteel Southern belle. Man, we tend to think, is basically good. If the world seems a mess, which it most usually does, the thing to do is not to belabor individuals, but rebuild human institutions.

In Bruegel's time, on the contrary, man—foolish, individual man—was still regarded as the culprit responsible for society's ills. The devil, to be sure, might be blamed for tempting man into committing one of the seven deadly sins. But the catalog of follies did not stop at seven. It was virtually endless. As Bruegel's age saw man, he was a feckless fellow who went blundering through life forever committing those foolish acts that a succession of pithy proverbs warned him against. He was always to be seen incorrigibly mistaking dung for diamonds, casting roses before swine, covering the well after the calf has fallen in, following blind men into a ditch and trying to squeeze blood out of a turnip.

Such proverbs were graphic. They could easily be painted. The actions shown were real and recognizable. But at the same time they were symbolic as well. The man covering the well after the calf has fallen in represented a general category of foolishness—the failure to take adequate precautions in time. These roughhewn symbols, the secular, low-brow counterparts of the sacred symbols so long used in religious paintings, were, in Bruegel's time and place, an almost universal way of seeing and summing up the nature of the world. Painters depicting a rowdy scene or a silly act could be sure that their audience, versed in the idiom of proverbs and symbols, was instantly prepared to "read" their meaning and would not only laugh, but get the moral message too.

The fashion of attacking folly began as pulpit oratory in the Middle Ages when clerics, using verse and sermon, established a tradition of berating the mighty for their abuses of the poor and of chiding the poor for their own foolishness. This mode of satiric social comment flourished throughout the 15th Century, but a decisive date in its development was the year 1496. In that year a Swiss poet named Sebastian Brant, armed with a catchy title and some telling woodcuts, launched *The Ship of Fools,* a book that dissected man's sorry condition in verse and pictures. Brant's glum nautical metaphor for society—which he saw as a cargo of fools, flatterers, gamblers, gossips, idlers and gluttons—had been used before by satirists, but his treatment of the theme caught the fancy of the age. *The Ship,* some of whose woodcuts may have been designed by Albrecht Dürer, was destined to be reprinted throughout Europe in 36 separate editions and half a dozen tongues. By 1500 collections of proverbs and illustrated lexicons of folly were sweeping Europe.

This literary fashion engaged even the talents of Erasmus of Rotterdam, the most prestigious philosopher of the age. In 1511, five years before the death of Bosch and a little more than a decade before Bruegel was born, the great humanist published *The Praise of Folly.* Earlier he had completed a book of adages, a collection in Latin and Greek of some 800

The custom of illustrating proverbs, adages and maxims was well established long before Bruegel took it up. An unknown French artist in the 15th Century made this pen-and-ink drawing as part of a manuscript collection of nearly 200 similar illustrations, each accompanied by a rhyme. The proverb here is, "In the country of the blind the one-eyed man is king."

sayings culled from the ancients. Erasmus by that time was already acclaimed throughout Europe as a counselor to kings and the man who had done most, as one historian put it, to "infuse a love for the beautiful and classic in place of the owlish pedantry which had so long flapped and hooted through medieval cloisters" in Europe. *The Praise of Folly* enjoyed fabulous success in its time—though its heavy-handed satiric method has little appeal for today's readers. Erasmus' literary device, telegraphed in the title, consisted in appearing to defend all sorts of follies while actually attacking the people who practice them. Flattery, he argued, far from being harmful, is really one of the useful elements from which human society is made. Where, he archly asked, would courts and kings, prelates and palaces, cities and governments be without it?

To a modern eye and ear, this treatment seems like little more than what, in fact, it was: one of the first academic "in" jokes of history. But to the 16th Century intellectual world, still partly mired in the deadly serious scholasticism of the waning Middle Ages, *The Praise of Folly* seemed very heady and revolutionary. Though a few academic numskulls failed to get the point (Erasmus had to write them and gently explain that he was really kidding), literate Europe as a whole was bowled over. Almost overnight the book confirmed Erasmus as a legendary character, a sort of combined Will Rogers, Marshall McLuhan and John Kenneth Galbraith to his age.

When it came to attacking human foolishness, Erasmus, Brant and many other collectors of proverbs, including a contemporary German mystic named Sebastian Franck, all had in common a kind of wry joviality. Their view was pessimistic—for they saw man as being incurably riddled with folly—but not depressed. "Whoever looks at mankind seriously," Franck once explained, may "break his heart with weeping"; but, Franck added, "We are all laughingstocks, fables and carnival farces before God." To dwell endlessly on the seven deadly sins and continually show corrupt sinners being flogged in hell, as Hieronymus Bosch had done, required an apocalyptic view and a temperament like Bosch's, easily prey to rage and despair. But to lampoon man's lesser follies by painting him in moments of foolishness (as when he belatedly covers his well or literally beats his head against a stone wall) required an eye for human foible more rueful than wrathful; a tone of voice, like Erasmus', less shrill than shrewd. This is the characteristic tone of Pieter Bruegel.

Flemish proverbs not only suited Bruegel's temper, they actually became part of his painting method. In the first years after his return from Rome, he turned out scores of drawings for various Hieronymus Cock print series on proverbs and executed a group of paintings, known today through copies probably made by Bruegel's son, showing 12 Flemish proverbs in miniature. Among them there is indeed a peasant stupidly beating his head against a wall and another man fruitlessly feeding roses to hogs. Both subjects turn up again in Bruegel's later drawings and paintings.

Bruegel's work was to mature in many ways. But the proverbs lingered on. Two of his last known paintings are *The Blind Leading the Blind* and *The Misanthrope (page 140)*, which shows a gloomy black-cloaked figure

Bruegel's earliest surviving design for engraving, completed about 1556, is a pen-and-ink drawing illustrating the temptations of St. Anthony. This engraving, published by the printer Hieronymus Cock, Bruegel's employer at the time, is based on the artist's drawing. It demonstrates how Bruegel used traditional Bible motifs and the popular legends of the lives of saints as a starting point for compositions filled with contemporary Flemish proverbs. A fuller explanation of the provocative imagery appears in the text on these pages.

having his pocket picked by a young thief who wears a circular metal frame (like a child's gyroscope) to indicate that he represents human behavior all over the globe. Together the two men represent a proverb in couplet form concerning a misanthrope and why he mourns over the ways of the world.

Bruegel put proverbs to many uses in the service of painting. Most often, as in *The Blind Leading the Blind,* a single proverb straightforwardly serves as title and subject for a single picture—sometimes with a little accompanying verse in Latin, French and Dutch. Occasionally proverbs are simply inserted into a larger scene to provide a bit of added "reading matter" for the viewer or an extra dimension of thought. Bruegel's large, late painting, *The Seastorm,* is a powerful and exciting view of sea, dark sky and wind-torn waves that is particularly prized today for its impressionistic rendering of stormy waters. But Bruegel (or his public) felt the need of a didactic message, so included in the picture is a small foundering ship and a rather silly-looking whale about to swallow a barrel that the crewmen have tossed overboard to distract the monster from the vessel itself. In the 16th Century the whale and the barrel constituted a well-known proverbial device for describing (and deploring) the behavior of men who turn aside from the main chances of life to snap up trumpery diversions.

Most often Bruegel used proverbs the way builders use bricks, as a basic unit of construction. How this works may best be seen in an en-

graving whose ostensible subject has nothing to do with proverbs whatever: *The Temptation of St. Anthony (opposite page)*. The subject was taken from *The Golden Legend* by Jacobus de Voragine, a 13th Century book that provided generations of artists and worshipers with fragmentary biographies of saints. In Bruegel's handling of the St. Anthony theme some of the elements are perfectly traditional. The old saint appears, as he often does in other pictures, kneeling in prayer and trying to keep his mind on the Scriptures despite the strange monsters that the devil has sent to distract him. But the rest of the Bruegel drawing is highly surrealistic: the vast, hollow, human head, with a huge fish fixed like a hat on top of it and with smoke pouring from its cavernous mouth; the eyeglasses stuck not on its nose but, like a pirate's ring, through one nostril; the tree branches, from one of which hangs a midget human figure with its head stuck in a sack, its legs wriggling in the air.

At first glance these oddities seem nightmarish and incomprehensible. But a study of the engraving's details reveals that it is really nothing more or less than a series of Flemish proverbs intertwined with one another and literally rendered. Trying to read it proverb by proverb is a bit like working out a Double-Crostic. To start with, the head is a standard Flemish symbol representing a special sort of folly. It is what was known as a *Peterskopf,* or hot-headed man (from St. Peter, who is characterized in the Bible as being inclined to impulsive rage). The smoke pouring from it can be traced to a pair of Flemish expressions. The first ("to make

This Bruegel engraving, like the print on the opposite page, depicts several interlocking Flemish proverbs. The basic maxim, "Big fish eat little fish," is illustrated by the grisly spectacle on the shore, where a flood of marine creatures, some disgorging others, spills from the gaping mouth and belly wound of a monster fish. The hooded man fishing at the right suggests a related saying— "Little fish lure the big"—while the symbol on the knife blade indicates the worldwide scope of man's voracious folly.

145

a man's head hot") means to anger him; the second ("When the head is full of smoke, no light can shine there") suggests that rage stifles intelligence. Additional details confirm that the head is indeed confused. One is the misplaced spectacles, for the Flemish say "first the nose and then the spectacles" to anyone who is putting the cart before the horse. The tiny man hanging from the tree branch with his head in a sack is another, since in German *Er hat den Kopf im Sack* is another way of saying "he doesn't know which end is up."

A clue to what the head and the fish in combination symbolize lies in a proverb adapted from the Greeks by Erasmus in his collection of adages. Erasmus' Latin rendering reads, "When the head is sick the whole body suffers"; an earthier Flemish version is harder hitting—"fish begin to rot at the head." Since the fish is also a traditional symbol of Christianity and the Roman Catholic Church, and the head clearly represents empty-headed human society (Flemish proverb: "His head is as hollow as an eggshell"), the two together can be interpreted as a visual allegory of the foolishness of human society in its subjection to the decaying authority of Rome. As if to clinch this interpretation, scholars have dug up an additional meaning for the fish. When Flemish peasants in Bruegel's time wanted to warn people not to be bamboozled or taken in, they said, "Don't let the herring swim over your head."

Even today some Dutch and Belgian Bruegel fanciers stand before the master's pictures quoting proverbs back and forth to see who can identify the most. For these few it is, as it was for Bruegel's contemporaries, relatively simple to decipher the proverbs and so read the painter's pictorial riddles right down to the fine print. But most modern Bruegel enthusiasts cannot cope with the content of many of his scenes without benefit of some sort of glossary of proverbs. Happily the artist provided just that, in *Netherlandish Proverbs (pages 151-159)*, one of his larger paintings (about four feet by five feet), nearly every square inch of which is devoted to scenes illustrating more than 100 proverbs. (The painting is also known as *The Blue Cloak* because of the man standing in the foreground with a blue cloak draped about his shoulders—a proverbial representation of that most foolish of figures, the cuckolded husband.)

According to a German proverb (not illustrated by Bruegel), "a country can be judged by the quality of its proverbs." Since proverbs—which go back at least to the Egyptian sage Ptah-Hotep in 3000 B.C.—have a way of turning up again and again from land to land, that proverb may not be wholly true. Bruegel's *Netherlandish Proverbs* certainly reveals that Flemish folk sayings had a flavor all their own—a flavor that is still retained in the proverbs of the modern language. They often tend toward a terse truculence: "There hangs the knife," for example, is a Flemish way of saying, "If you want to start something, buddy, you know where to begin." They lend tired, old international favorites fresh graphic verve: "Don't count your chickens before they're hatched" becomes, "An eel caught by the tail is only half caught." Above all they are earthy. No Fleming, apparently, ever called a spade a spade if he could possibly call it a manure fork.

Besides conveying the pungent flavor of his country's folk sayings,

Bruegel's *Proverbs* also serves as a kind of Rosetta stone, which can help reveal the mysteries of his work as a whole. The picture is packed with proverbs, like "big fish eat little fish" and "the blind leading the blind," which Bruegel returned to throughout his painting lifetime. Moreover, in a rough-and-ready way the painting provides miniature color previews of the physical world, which the painter was eventually to create in his later paintings—glimpses of rich warm fields of wheat, tiny estuaries on which small fishing boats with leg-of-mutton sails glide like leaves, thatched roofs, smoking chimneys and scores of antlike people.

The compositional form used in *Proverbs* is known as *Wimmelbild* (literally, "teeming figure picture") in which masses of small figures are presented on a large painting surface, seen from above as a Coney Island beach crowd might be seen from a low-flying helicopter. Bruegel used the form often, particularly for popular mass pictures like *Proverbs* and *Children's Games.* Technically, the great difficulty with a picture of this type lies in keeping it from looking cluttered. Many of Bruegel's contemporaries and successors who painted *Wimmelbilder* failed to do so. As executed by someone like Hans Bol, for instance, a younger contemporary of Bruegel's, a typical village square choked with townsfolk looks very choked indeed. Figures overlap one another; heads, arms and legs get jumbled up in a confused clutter or seem to sprout from the wrong bodies. Confronted with such a disorderly mass, the eye grows tired.

One of Bruegel's greatest achievements as a painter was his skillful avoidance of such confusion. His success in this, as in much else, lay in his ability to blend old and new painting traditions. Before Bruegel, most Flemish artists avoided clutter when presenting a large number of human figures by largely ignoring the rules of perspective. Figures did not overlap, for instance, as they do in real life but were spotted around the painting like decorations on a rug. The scene itself was presented as a flat surface, and little effort was made to convey a sense of distance with receding lines of sight or foreshortening. By Bruegel's time, however, most painters had begun to feel obliged to present crowds of people according to the rules of realism and perspective. The results seem authentic enough but, as in Bol's works, they look crowded—because bodies and groups get in each other's way, as they do in real life, and individual details are lost as objects get progressively farther from the eye.

Almost alone among painters, Bruegel combined the archaic approach with the new science of perspective. To create the illusion of perspective he leads the eye into the depths of the picture with lines created by village streets or the façades of houses. But he avoids letting his figures be obscured by overlapping and by the effects of distance, as they would be in reality, by tipping his landscape up as it recedes. That is, he appears to move his vantage point progressively higher as the picture recedes. As a result, the figures and groups in the background are not blocked from view by groups in front of them. In addition, he usually painted these background figures larger than they would appear under the normal rules of perspective.

The pleasure of looking at Bruegel's large, teeming pictures is not just an esthetic one. It also involves natural delight at being able to observe

These two, small wood carvings, called misericords after the Latin word for mercy, are decorations attached to the bottom sides of seats in the choir stalls of a 15th Century Belgian church. The seats were turned up while clergy and singers stood through lengthy services, and these misericords—found in many churches of the time—provided merciful supports to lean back upon. The carvings illustrate two Flemish proverbs that were popular in Bruegel's day. At the top, the napping monk suggests that "a good conscience makes the best pillow." Below, the foolish jester reveals that "he who would outyawn the stove must yawn long," a proverb that Bruegel himself illustrated in the painting discussed on pages 152-157.

the details of a complete world in miniature, because Bruegel has borrowed the technique of a miniature painter in taking minute care to capture the realistic details of scores of interrelated homey vignettes. But the world thus created by Bruegel is not exactly the same as the real-life scene that a camera could render more swiftly and accurately. It is an imaginary creation with convincing details, which, like the rooms of a skillfully created doll house, satisfyingly create the illusion of reality.

Unlike the beautiful illusions of the real world created by the 19th Century French Impressionist painters, however, Bruegel's visions will bear close scrutiny. If you move close to a painting by Claude Monet or Camille Pissarro, the vision of reality fragments. You find yourself face to face not with nature but with painting technique—the meaningless brushstrokes, the flecks and dashes of color that at a distance admirably convey a unified impression of the world. Bruegel never does your seeing for you. The closer you get to one of his pictures, the more of his world you are invited to examine. The eye can rove happily on and on, relishing new forms and faces. The mind can reflect on the possibility, often conveyed by miniaturist paintings, that if the viewer could just push open the door of that thatched hut there in the background, or stumble into the alehouse here in the near foreground, he would find himself in a complete, three-dimensional world. At the very least the inhabitants might be found frozen in place—like the people in Sleeping Beauty's castle—needing only a human intrusion to wake them into life.

If Bruegel's didactic paintings are set about with realistic houses, wells and sheds, his rendering of people ranges from realistic clumsiness to cruel caricature in which limbs appear more lumpish, faces more brutish, eyes more greedy and lecherous than they customarily are in reality. Any art form devoted to lampooning human folly naturally gives a painter license to exaggerate the cloddishness of man at his everyday worst, and Bruegel certainly took advantage of that license. Nevertheless it is a great temptation, especially in an age like ours, which assumes that painters exercise complete personal choice about what they paint, to wonder if Bruegel's portraits of human folly do not reveal his private feelings and to conclude that those feelings reflect a personal distaste for man akin to the revulsion felt by the 18th Century Irish satirist Jonathan Swift. One feels certain from reading *Gulliver's Travels* that Swift saw everyday men as greedy, violent, smelly, ignorant creatures like those whom the book's civilized creatures, the horselike Houyhnhnms, refer to as Yahoos. Many of Bruegel's portraits are just as unflattering. One of the unkindest is a drawing—which survives only as a print—called *Elck,* the Flemish word for Everyman. It is a complicated picture with many figures, all of them drawn to represent the same bewhiskered, long-nosed man, who is stirring about, hunting with lanterns through the piled up goods of the world that lie about him. *Elck,* the caption explains in Flemish, French and Latin, is greedy man, always self-seeking but never self-knowing.

Is *Elck* Bruegel's private view of mankind? We cannot know. For unlike Swift, who was creating his own imagery in an original satiric form, Bruegel, in *Elck,* was working within the confines of traditional subjects. As such, it was not necessarily a statement of personal conviction. The peculiar power of Bruegel's didactic pictures, in any case, does not depend on their message but on their artistic achievement. Bruegel painted proverbs, drew human caricatures and exposed man's folly with more vitality and in more compelling detail than anyone in his or any other age. In doing so he raised instructive painting from the level of propaganda to the rank of universal art.

For a hint of Bruegel's personal estimate of his fellow man it is necessary to find a painting that Bruegel seems to handle in a uniquely personal way. One such picture is *Landscape with the Fall of the Icarus (page 160)*. The Greek myth about a rash boy who is given wax wings by his father, Daedalus, and who pridefully flies too close to the sun and so falls to his death in the sea has always intrigued artists; one reason for its interest to Bruegel was the rising popularity of classical themes, and another was the fact that Icarus' tragedy has a built-in didactic moral about the disaster that pride inevitably brings down upon man.

Bruegel deliberately changed the message by painting Icarus as nobody else ever has. He does not use the rich, somber hues of the North, as was his wont, but instead deals in the radiant dawn colors of the Mediterranean world. A distant sun glows white on a blue-green sea, washing the white shapes of a distant city, silvering the masts of a stately ship whose sails are fat with wind. Like many other painters, Bruegel peopled the scene with characters ashore and afloat—a ship at sea, and on shore a plowman following his horse, an idle shepherd boy, an old fisherman. One difference in Bruegel's vision of the scene is that Icarus himself is barely noticeable. He is shown just hitting the water, and his legs and a tiny splash are all that can be seen of him in the sea near the shore. But the most important difference of all is that everyone ignores his fall. The ploughman, the fisherman, the boy go casually about their affairs. Nobody is looking. By painting the picture in this eccentric way, Bruegel has transformed the myth into a proverb. Now its message, as one art historian put it, is, "A man dies, and the world hardly blinks."

A more eloquent description of the painting and perhaps a more generous interpretation of its implications was made by W. H. Auden, in a poem written after seeing *Landscape with the Fall of Icarus* hanging in the Royal Museum in Brussels:

> About suffering they were never wrong,
> The Old Masters: how well they understood
> Its human position; how it takes place
> While someone else is eating or opening a window or just
> walking dully along; . . .
>
> In Brueghel's Icarus, for instance: how everything turns away
> Quite leisurely from the disaster; the ploughman may
> Have heard the splash, the forsaken cry,
> But for him it was not an important failure; the sun shone
> As it had to on the white legs disappearing into the green
> Water; and the expensive delicate ship that must have seen
> Something amazing, a boy falling out of the sky,
> Had somewhere to get to and sailed calmly on.

A Panoply of Proverbs

Imagine a world beset by folly, where proverbial absurdities are literally acted out. That is the world exposed in Bruegel's painting *The Blue Cloak,* whose appropriate central image *(opposite)* is a buxom, adulterous wife hiding her infidelities from her cuckold husband in an enveloping blue cloak—blue commonly symbolized deceit or lying in 16th Century Flanders. As this keynote suggests, Bruegel's foolish world is not imaginary but real—he has clothed it in the trappings of a Flemish village. The streets and barnyards are filled with more than a hundred details and vignettes, each illustrating a different Netherlandish proverb.

On the pages that follow, Bruegel's remarkable painting is closely examined. Not surprisingly, many of the proverbs that were familiar to Bruegel's audience are still in use today. Old saws such as the overcautious warrior who is actually armed to the teeth, or the deceitful man who speaks with two separate mouths, are pictured with graphic exactness. It was Bruegel's genius that he could with such imagination illustrate those verbal images that make language so rich and man's reflections on his own poor fate so rueful and pithy. In the words of one of Bruegel's contemporaries, the German writer Sebastian Franck, "We are all laughingstocks, fables and carnival plays before God." And in Bruegel's telling, this black comedy of 16th Century life becomes as pertinent as the most biting political cartoon in today's paper.

Like the key melody in a song, this homely detail sets the tone for Bruegel's scene—probably the first of his large pictures to teem with human activities. The tradition of illustrating proverbs was old in Bruegel's time; engravings, tapestries and paintings of one or more sayings or homilies had long been known. But never had any artist orchestrated them in a large work with such inventiveness and pictorial skill.

Fascinated by the compendium of folklore, rhymes, symbols and maxims contained in *The Blue Cloak,* art historians have engaged in a vigorous and protracted guessing game to identify them all. Many references are obscure today, some would be recognized only by European readers and others are frankly scatological. A selection of the most amusing and familiar ones appears in the list below, which is keyed to the numbered diagram above. The areas outlined in white correspond to the full color double-page reproductions on the following pages.

1 Tarts on the roof (symbol of plenty)
2 There hangs the knife (a challenge)
3 The fool gets the trump card (fortune favors fools)
4 They lead one another by the nose
5 The cross hangs beneath the orb (it's a topsy-turvy world)
6 To send one arrow after the other (to throw good after bad)
7 An old roof needs much repair
8 He has a toothache behind his ear (to fool others by malingering)
9 The roof has laths (there are eavesdroppers)
10 He speaks out of two mouths

Pages 154-155
11 She would bind the devil himself (the devil,

like a naughty child, is tied to a pillow)
12 The pillar-biter (a man so hypocritically pious that he even embraces church pillars)
13 The hat on the pillar (literally something under one's hat, a secret)
14 She carries fire in one hand, water in the other (contradictory opinions)
15 He cooks herring for the sake of the roes (to do things in a roundabout way)
16 He bangs his head against the wall
17 The sow removes the spigot (to make a pig of oneself)
18 He bells the cat (armed to the teeth, he is brave enough for the task)
19 Don't count your chickens before they're hatched
20 He always gnaws at one bone (he plays

only one tune)
21 There hang the scissors (sign of the pickpocket)
22 One shears the sheep, the other the pig (pig shearing yields no wool)
23 Patient as a lamb
24 One holds the distaff while the other spins (it takes two to gossip)
25 He carries baskets of light out into the sunshine (coals to Newcastle)

Pages 156-157
26 She hangs a blue cloak (lies) around her husband
27 He fills in the well after the calf has drowned (locking the barn door after the horse has gone)

The Blue Cloak (The Netherlandish Proverbs), 1559

28 A man must stoop low if he wishes to get through the world (to accommodate oneself to conditions)
29 He casts roses (pearls) before swine
30 The pig's stuck through the belly (it is irrevocable)
31 To have the devil for a confessor
32 An ear-blower (a gossip)
33 The fox dines with the crane (an unlikely pair, an image from Aesop's fables)
34 A sponge-spoon (a sponger)
35 What good is a beautiful plate if it is empty?
36 Two dogs over one bone rarely agree (bone of contention)
37 He sits on hot coals (is on tenter-hooks)
38 He gives the Lord a flaxen beard (mockery)
39 The world turns on his thumb (he's got the world on a string)
40 To poke a stick into the wheel
41 They pull for the long piece (a game in which a pretzel, like a wishbone, is pulled apart for luck)
42 He who spills his gruel can't get it all up (no use crying over spilt milk)
43 He cannot reach from one loaf to the other (make ends meet)
44 A hoe without a handle (a useless thing)
45 He who would outyawn the stove must yawn long (a senseless endeavor)
46 He sits in his own light (basks in his glory)
47 She takes the hen's egg and leaves the goose's (to make a bad choice)
48 He hangs between heaven and hell

Pages 158-159
49 He catches fish with his hands (is very clever)
50 Big fish eat little fish
51 He fishes behind the net (wasted effort)
52 Two fools beneath one cap (stupidity loves company)
53 On a fool's beard, the barber learns to shave
54 It grows out of the window (the secret cannot be kept quiet)
55 He fiddles in the pillory (to dance on the gallows)
56 The pigs run loose in the corn (everything has gone wrong)
57 He falls from the ox to the ass (to go from good to bad)
58 He opens the door with his backside (he doesn't know whether he's coming or going)
59 Anyone can see through an oak door if there is a hole in it
60 He throws his money into the water

61 He resents the sun shining on the water (he is so stingy that he even resents the sun)
62 An eel held by the tail is not yet caught
63 The broadest straps are cut from someone else's hides (to risk someone else's skin)
64 It is hard to swim against the tide
65 He throws his cowl over the fence (gives up the vows of Holy Orders—poverty, chastity, obedience)
66 He sees the bears dancing (is hungry)
67 He doesn't care whose house is burning as long as he can warm himself from the coals
68 He kills two flies with one blow
69 She gazes after the stork (has nothing better to do)
70 He hangs his cloak according to the wind (an opportunist)
71 He pours feathers out into the wind (a senseless activity)
72 He is dragging the block (heavy-hearted)
73 Only fear makes the old lady run
74 If the blind lead the blind both shall fall into the ditch
75 Horse manure is not figs
76 It is easiest to sail before the wind
77 He has one eye on the sail (stays alert)
78 Who knows why the geese walk barefoot?

153

154

Landscape with the Fall of Icarus, c.1558

Musée des Beaux Arts

W. H. AUDEN

About suffering they were never wrong,
The Old Masters: how well they understood
Its human position; how it takes place
While someone else is eating or opening a window or just
    walking dully along;
How, when the aged are reverently, passionately waiting
For the miraculous birth, there always must be
Children who did not specially want it to happen, skating
On a pond at the edge of the wood:
They never forgot
That even the dreadful martyrdom must run its course
Anyhow in a corner, some untidy spot

Where the dogs go on with their doggy life and the
    torturer's horse
Scratches its innocent behind on a tree.

In Brueghel's Icarus, for instance: how everything turns away
Quite leisurely from the disaster; the ploughman may
Have heard the splash, the forsaken cry,
But for him it was not an important failure; the sun shone
As it had to on the white legs disappearing into the green
Water; and the expensive delicate ship that must have seen
Something amazing, a boy falling out of the sky,
Had somewhere to get to and sailed calmly on.

VII

Painter of Work and Weather

If many aspects of life and learning have changed beyond recognition since Pieter Bruegel's time, the landscape of much of the world has not. Painters no longer deal in proverbs. Flowing robes have shrunk to mini-skirts. Once quaint Flemish cities have turned into soot-filled factory sites. But trees are still trees, and there are still pleasant corners of the earth where hills and fields and streams reassuringly meet the eye as they did in the 16th Century.

It would be reasonable to expect that landscape has always been a popular subject for art and equally natural to assume that countryside has been painted in very much the same way from century to century. However, quite the contrary is true. Through much of its early history, landscape painting was scoffed at by the movers and shapers of artistic fashion. To a religious age, after all, what was a plowed field or a stand of chestnut trees compared to the Birth of Christ or the Fall of Man? Even when the category of accepted subjects for art broadened in the Renaissance to embrace the human as well as the divine comedy, pure countryside could hardly compete for space with the new interest in heroic myth, great historic moments and the ennoblement of the human figure.

Michelangelo spoke for the Renaissance in general when he critically referred to the type of landscape painting favored by the Flemish as stuff fit only for "young women, monks, nuns and certain noble persons with no sense of true harmony."

The Flemish inclination toward landscape painting that Michelangelo found so trivial went back to the early 1300s, to the tiny calendar scenes in the Books of Hours, where a single month might be illustrated by a sliver of background landscape. The painting of calendar scenes for the Books of Hours continued for the next two centuries, but during that time landscape was to flourish mainly within the shadow of sacred subject matter, so that during this time the evolution of Flemish landscape painting can hardly be separated from the growth of its religious art.

It was Jan van Eyck who first gave a brilliant place to countryside in Flemish oil painting when he created a huge altarpiece for the Church of

St. Bavon in Ghent. Done in 1432, the multi-paneled painting portrays an Annunciation, the figures of Adam and Eve and likenesses of the donor and his wife. Its central panel, though, is devoted to the Lamb of God, shown standing on an altar surrounded by adoring choirs of saints and richly clad angels. Beyond the Lamb, Van Eyck painted in soft undulating fields dotted like tapestries with orderly trees, precise shrubs and perfectly petaled flowers, which lead the eye away from the green foreground into the hazy distance.

From the very beginning the *Ghent Altarpiece* was a showpiece and a touchstone of art. Men journeyed from all over northern Europe to marvel at its blend of religious symbol and realistic detail, to study its subtle workings of light and shadow and to revel in the delicious softness of its landscape greenery. Even as late as 1604 Van Mander could still report that "painters swarm around it like summer flies around a basket of figs and grapes."

Starting with Van Eyck and the *Ghent Altarpiece,* a steady flirtation with natural countryside in ostensibly religious art set in among Flemish oil painters. For a time it could only be fleetingly pursued. Flowery fields and sylvan glades could be enjoyed, so to speak, only behind the back of the Blessed Virgin, or of Joseph and the assembled kings and shepherds in innumerable Nativities and Adorations. Such brief glimpses of landscape are immeasurably attractive, but, gilded by benevolent sunlight and decked out with porcelain-bright flowers, they present a vision of the world that owes more to the Garden of Eden than to the country around Ghent or any other Flemish town.

The pleasantly profane is always likely to catch the popular eye, and very gradually delectable countryside began displacing Christianity in religious painting. Trees and fields took up more and more space; the Biblical figures less. Even so, the change was neither rapid nor steady, but it is clear enough, and occasionally accompanied by a breakthrough in the direction of rustic realism. One historic landmark, ironically, is an actual background portrait of the Garden of Eden that occurs in Hugo Van der Goes' *Fall of Man,* painted around 1467. Van der Goes' major concern is still thoroughly Biblical. The strongest pictorial thrust of his picture is provided by the awkward, naked figures of Adam and Eve with their Tempter, standing on stumpy hind legs. Around this Biblical trio, however, the Garden of Eden no longer resembles a stylized heaven on earth. A few trees and flowers still have a manicured, hothouse look. But the surrounding countryside as a whole swoops freely away in the background, up a wooded slope with rough, open patches that make it look like a slightly overgrown New England pasture.

Despite the increased painting space devoted to them, and despite isolated sorties like that of Van der Goes in the direction of the realistic scenery, the exact contours of everyday countryside were not to become the subject of Biblical landscape for a while yet. Painters did not move outdoors to paint at easels until the 18th Century. Landscape backgrounds, like the other elements in early Flemish painting, were worked up in the studio—only rarely on the basis of outdoor sketches, most often as a mixture of memory, imagination and painting convention. When in the early 1500s the Garden of Eden style finally did give way for good, it was replaced by another artistic convention, something equally attractive but also largely unreal.

By this time Flemish artists were feeling the influence of the Italian Renaissance passion for space and its accompanying preoccupation with rules of perspective. They were also living in an expanding world. Great map makers, correlating the discoveries of the age of exploration, were turning out globe-girdling projections. Bird's-eye renderings of famous cities, like those still sold today, were just coming into fashion—maplike creations in which rows of houses sketched in perspective were superimposed upon the actual street plans of great capitals like Venice and Paris.

Partly as a reflection of this newly grasped sense of the vastness and variety of the earth, painters began increasing the space and depth of their landscape backgrounds. To get distance required height. Religious paintings soon began to look as if they had been painted by a man surveying the world from an immensely high cliff. Religious figures were painted into the foreground on a ledge or hill. Beyond them, customarily, there would be a great drop to a lower plane, where the shires of the world stretched toward a distant, high horizon. This artistic convention, which seemed to encompass the extreme limits of the earth, became known as "cosmic" or "universal" landscape.

The Garden of Eden style had led 15th Century Flemish painters toward the use of dainty, bucolic details; the new universal landscape produced not only a more expansive vision of the land, but also one full of curious inconsistencies. Both the incongruities of style and the spacious beauty of the new form are best illustrated in the work of Joachim Patinir, the one man who was almost as important to Flemish landscape painting as Pieter Bruegel.

An Antwerp master who died in 1524, within a year or two of Bruegel's birth, Patinir was by far the most influential and gifted practitioner of cosmic landscape. He was also the first painter ever to become famous solely on the basis of his skill at landscape. Patinir cared so little for depicting the human form that he often had the necessary Biblical figures painted into his landscapes by other artists—most notably his versatile contemporary, Quentin Massys. The figures in Patinir's landscapes grew steadily smaller during his lifetime until, in *Sodom and Gomorrah,* one of his last and most spectacular pictures, he concentrated so completely upon showing the countryside and the burning of the iniquitous city that Lot and his family and the two angels sent to guide them to safety are so small as to be barely visible.

In some Patinir pictures, traces of Garden of Eden greenery still linger —especially in the foregrounds around the Virgin or St. Jerome or whatever devotional character he has chosen to neglect. But Patinir's backgrounds become more and more bizarre. Anyone who could stroll into the depths of a Patinir landscape would find himself stumbling among strange stage sets and oddly juxtaposed chunks of terrain in a kind of natural Disneyland. Praying hermits and peasant hamlets nestle among gentle hills. Stands of oak grow beside an occasional palm tree. Bunny rabbits browse with camels—the latter being most useful symbolic beasts whose presence indicated to viewers that the action was taking place somewhere in the Holy Land. Patinir found room for Gothic chapels and bristling battlements and a peculiar round-domed temple, which he and other painters employed to represent Jerusalem's Church of the Holy Sepulchre. Most of all, however, Patinir's universal landscape can be recognized by great outcroppings of rock—some exploding toward heaven like monstrous granite ears—and by vast river deltas winding away through the blue distance to a hazy and imaginary sea.

The heir to this splendid fantasy terrain was Bruegel. Patinir had given landscape new cosmic scope, but he never quite freed himself of the need to include religious or classical figures in his scenery. Bruegel was to do so, painting countryside for its own sake and raising landscape to heights of artistry never achieved before his time. To gain space for scenery in religious art, Patinir had reduced his Biblical figures to Lilliputian proportions. Bruegel, finding his models in the peasants in the Books of Hours, dealt with everyday man, restoring him to normal size and presenting him at work in the natural world. In thus boldly hanging a "Men at Work" sign on Patinir's cosmic Netherlandish scenery, Bruegel more than any other painter helped free landscape from its dependence on religion. More important, he created a handful of original landscape scenes that have achieved an enduring place above and beyond the ebb and flow of art fashion and art history.

From the very beginning Bruegel's work combined a strong inclination toward natural scenery with a craftsman's debt to Patinir. Many of the landscape drawings that Bruegel executed for Hieronymus Cock after his return from Italy in 1553 support Van Mander's theory that Bruegel had sketched his way through alpine countryside. But many more, cast in the compositional mold of Patinir's universal landscape, could have served as preliminary sketches for pictures by the earlier painter.

Patinir's influence did not stop with the drawings. The painting *Landscape with Christ Appearing to the Apostles* might also be taken for his work were it not signed by Bruegel and dated 1553. Nearly half of Bruegel's surviving pictures can be classified as landscapes of one sort or another, and a surprising percentage of them, like *Landscape with the Parable of the Sower* and even the relatively late *Landscape with the Flight into Egypt,* apparently painted in 1563, are highly derivative.

It was characteristic of Bruegel to support himself on the long road toward the creation of pioneering landscapes by picking the artistic pockets of his predecessors. But as he worked his way through predictable topics he gradually began to modify them to suit his own genius, first in manner, finally in matter. Nothing could be more traditional in subject and composition than the *Flight Into Egypt.* There are the tiny figures of Mary and Joseph on a foreground hill. There are improbably jagged rock cliffs thrusting up into the middle distance. There is the far-off sea. Nevertheless, the Bruegelian landscape miracle is beginning to take place. What is essentially fantasy landscape is being transformed by art into something that bears, if not the shape, at least the colors and textures of reality. The rough, spiky tip of a dead hemlock tree sticks up from below a foreground hill to link the near and far sections of the picture. Bruegel has got away, once and for all, from Patinir's bright, smooth colors and his decorative trees, leaves and hills with outlines as sharp as if cut by a jeweler's tool. In their place Bruegel has used a softer, freer line and the shaggy, mellow hues and surfaces of real countryside.

In the process of eliminating the sacred elements from his landscapes, Bruegel experimented with new variations on the subject. Today the display rooms of most Dutch and Belgian museums give much wall space to two kinds of paintings whose most celebrated ancestors were created in Bruegel's atelier. Seascapes with shipping, for example, the half-sisters of landscape (also called "marine landscapes") have been a Netherlandish specialty since the early 17th Century. But the first important examples were created 50 years before that by Bruegel when he painted the *View of the Harbor of Naples* and *The Seastorm*.

Another characteristic subject of Dutch painting is the agreeably crowded skating scene. Along with seascapes, they suddenly bloomed like tulips in the rising sun of middle-class popularity in the early 1600s, represented by the work of Dutch masters like Hendrik Avercamp and Jan van Goyen. Yet it was Bruegel, probably early in 1565, who created the first dazzling example—a small, exquisite, pearly-hued picture called *Winter Scene with Skaters and Bird Trap,* which shows a frozen Flemish stream lined with dark, snow-trimmed trees and populated by a scattering of skaters under a somber sky. (Not only did the theme become popular, but this picture itself was perpetuated in the next generation. An almost exact copy of it *(page 184)* was painted several decades later by Pieter Bruegel the Younger.)

The year 1565 was a portentous one in the history of landscape painting, for it was then that Bruegel drew together all the threads of past artistic practice and wove them into an unforgettable tapestry of man, earth and the returning seasons. Weather, like work, had been lacking from both the Garden of Eden landscapes of the 15th Century and Patinir's cosmic views. Now Bruegel set out to create a landscape series showing the working man touched by the cycle of the seasons *(pages 174-183)*. Preparing them, he did what no painter had done before him—he used for massive and detailed inspiration the calendar illustrations from the traditional Flemish Books of Hours.

The series was almost certainly commissioned by Bruegel's wealthy patron, Niclaes Jonghelinck, who had bought a mansion on the outskirts of Antwerp and sought to decorate it with the work of contemporary artists. It is not known how many landscapes were commissioned—only five still exist—and Bruegel did not give them titles. But they have become famous under descriptive titles acquired in succeeding centuries: *Hunters in the Snow, The Dark Day, The Harvesters, The Hay Harvest* and *The Return of the Herd.*

Calendar illustrations in the Books of Hours customarily represented the games and chores of each of the 12 months separately. But sometimes for pictorial purposes it was possible to combine them into two-month periods, with six pictures illustrating the seasonal activities of a whole year. In his seasonal cycle Bruegel probably shifted some traditional chores around. He certainly modified some and added a few that had

The accurate details of the sails and rigging in this handsome print, one of 13 ship engravings known to have been designed by Bruegel, indicate that the artist turned his acute powers of observation as searchingly on the sea and its ships as he did on his native countryside. He has illustrated here a three-masted galleon, a heavily armed warship of the type that guarded Flanders' trade routes during the 16th Century. The smaller ship is a galley similar to those seen in the Mediterranean, which may have been used as a "water taxi" in the Low Countries.

never been used in art before. He also aimed at more than mere decorative documentation of the outdoor work of any given month. What he was reaching for, and achieved, were total portraits of the seasons, from the changing of the land to the look of a day. It is difficult, therefore, to be doctrinaire about just how many paintings Bruegel's original series included. Still, on the basis of the five that survive, it seems likely that he confined his sequential portrait of the outdoor year to six pictures covering two months each—which could mean that only the April-May picture is now missing.

The foreground of *Hunters in the Snow* (December-January) includes a group of peasants singeing off pig bristles—a variation on the hog butchering theme that often appeared in the calendar illustrations—but the dominant subject of the painting is really winter itself and the somber figures of tired hunters trudging home ahead of a pack of doleful dogs. *The Dark Day* focuses on a traditional scene for February and March—peasants trimming willow trees—and its place in the yearly cycle is further fixed by the presence of a boy munching on a special kind of waffle baked only at Mardi Gras time. Most convincing is the mood of the picture itself. The view lifts toward a distant seascape where a gale-force wind is kicking up whitecaps and sinking ships, and the whole work breathes the blustery mood of early March. The picture that perhaps owes most to the Books of Hours activities is *The Harvesters* (August-September), which shows a whole spectrum of peasant humanity at work, mowing and stacking wheat, eating and drowsing between bouts of work. The least traditional is the final scene, *The Return of the Herd* (October-November). Choosing his own representative chore, Bruegel, for the first time in seasonal landscape painting, links autumnal hues with the fall's work of driving down the cows from their summer pasturage on the high slopes to their winter quarters in a mountain village.

Little enough is known about Bruegel's circumstances, but we know more about him during the year 1565 than at any other period of his life. Apparently, the circumstances of that year conspired in various ways to ensure that the new landscape series would be among his greatest works. He was about 40 years old and at the height of his powers. Forty was relatively older then than it is now, but then as now it was a time when men look backward to take stock of what lies behind them and, if they have been doing well, feel a warming sense of mastery in their work, which gives them confidence. Although the times were troubled (religious riots had already broken out by then, and it would be barely two years before Alba's army began laying waste the Low Countries) Bruegel was clearly doing well.

The Jonghelinck commission was a fat one. Prices were related to the size of paintings, and these would be among the largest Bruegel ever painted—each one more than three feet by five feet. Besides, the Antwerp merchant was probably prepared to spend good money for his art. (In addition to Bruegel he seems to have hired the fashionable and expensive Frans Floris to help decorate the new mansion.) Bruegel had been settled in Brussels for three years after his migration from Antwerp, and he was living with his new young wife Mayken and their firstborn, one-year-old Pieter. Whatever his religious persuasion, the painter must have felt securely grateful to be embarking on a subject like the seasons—well paid, and so completely secular that neither hot-eyed Calvinist nor cold Inquisitor could possibly object to it.

The paintings were probably designed to hang in the same room in Jonghelinck's house and be viewed as an orchestrated frieze with a more or less unified effect. Four out of the five surviving pictures are signed and dated 1565. Both these factors suggest a number of things about the way the series was composed and painted.

To do so much within one year (for he painted a number of other pictures as well) Bruegel must have worked very fast, with a sureness of hand and eye rarely surpassed in art. Paint dried slowly and each panel took many coats. To save time painters often worked on several paintings at once. Both for this reason and because he needed to be sure of the total impact of the pictures as a group, it is probable that Bruegel planned the whole series, down to details of color and composition, before putting brush to paint. Having done so he must have then set up all six panels— if indeed there were six—in his studio at once and worked on them in turn, switching from one to another to let each successive coat of paint dry properly.

The pictures were done on oak panels that had been aged ten years in their preparation as painting surfaces. Each panel was first primed with a white, chalky coat of fine white plaster and glue. Then, to serve as the delicate skeleton of the future painting, came thin, dark outlines of trees, human figures and countryside. The surfaces were slowly built up, layer by layer, with each coat of paint showing through the next to modify its color slightly until a final effect was achieved that would be quite unmatchable by simply trying to blend the proper colors directly from the pigments. In *Hunters in the Snow,* for instance, it is early coats of a startling lemon yellow glowing through many layers put on later that lend luminous inner warmth to the solid brown fronts of the peasant houses in the left foreground.

It was the drying that took the longest. As the weeks passed, waiting for the surfaces to harden properly, overseeing the grinding of pigment, clipping his smallest brushes down to a mere whisker to trace the finest details, Bruegel gradually immersed himself in the colors of the turning year: snowy whites and wintry blues; the red-black of trees through which early sap is stirring; the blue-greens of fresh, young summer grasses churned by scythe strokes and flailing pitchforks; the flat golds of August where a whole landscape drowses under a thick sunlight that dulls both the pale straw stubble and the rich ocher of uncut wheat; finally the rusts and smoky grays of fall in the high mountains. So, encircled by the seasons, returning again and again to each in turn, the artist must have watched his six pictures blossom slowly under his hand, from the bare oak panels to the finished products.

When Bruegel began the series he was entering upon the last and greatest phase of his painting life. Only four years were left to him, but he filled them with a succession of fine and philosophic works—in most of which, landscape or not, he continued the practice of introducing

ÆTAS ARGENTEA.

Tobias Verhaecht inuent.
Ioan. Collaert Sculp.

Ioan. Galle excude. Cum.

A vivid picture of life on a 16th Century Flemish farm is provided by this curious engraving—though its ostensible subject is a picture of life during the mythical Age of Silver, when Zeus ruled, men lived by the fruits of their labor and luxury prevailed. The scene was designed by the Flemish landscape painter Tobias Verhaecht, who was Peter Paul Rubens' first master, and the engraving was made about 1600. It shows a fantasy landscape filled with a meticulously drawn inventory of farm tools, animals and implements: a plow, scythe, rake, flail, spade and reed basket; cows, sheep, oxen, goats and pigs; and a fish weir straddling a stream where a woman washes clothes.

weather and often human labor as well. The pictures of this period include *Peasant Wedding,* for instance, and most of the Biblical scenes that tease us with possible political implications. But with the completion of the seasons Bruegel had reached one pinnacle of his creative lifetime and brought one form of painting to a level that it had never before reached and in a sense was never to reach again.

The universal appeal of the landscape series is extraordinary. It also, in large measure, defies logical explanation. Anyone can easily trace to their sources Bruegel's innumerable borrowings—from the immense foreground-to-background reach of Patinir's cosmic landscapes to the rustic pastimes lifted from the Books of Hours. Art experts are fond of pointing out, too, that Bruegel's use of perspective is not quite consistent. If you walked down the foreground hill in *Hunters in the Snow,* for example, and out onto the ice of the nearest pond, the human figures there, as Bruegel painted them, would actually turn out to be about the size of rabbits.

These observations underline an interesting fact. Bruegel's landscapes are not replicas of any real scene. They are studio paintings, fantasy creations patched together from bits of scenery, much of which Bruegel never saw, let alone sketched: imaginary seas, cliffs that never existed and Flemish houses that did. *The Return of the Herd* may just possibly be a re-creation from sketches and 12-year-old memories of mountain scenes encountered by Bruegel in the Alps on his way to or from Rome. But as totalities, the other views did not exist anywhere in Flanders or in Europe. They are, in one sense, as wholly imaginary as the strange, infernal terrains created by Hieronymus Bosch.

None of this seems to make any difference. The pictures are irresistibly appealing. It is impossible for us not to marvel at their authenticity and to believe—in a profound and satisfying, though thoroughly illogical way—that the land and the people they show once existed, just as Bruegel painted them.

Examining why Bruegel's landscapes look so real, when by rights they should not, one naturally begins by ticking off a list of lovely and convincingly realistic details used by the painter. In *Hunters in the Snow,* for instance, there is a line of smoke-puff bushes, silently exploding like gray cotton shellfire in the winter stillness. Faithfully recorded in *The Return of the Herd* is the simple fact that autumn leaves fall from trees high on an alpine slope long before they do in the warmer valleys below. Another Bruegelian accuracy is a miraculous truthfulness of light and atmosphere best illustrated by the compelling darkness of the particular kind of March afternoon that provides the title of *The Dark Day.*

Even when this has been said, the reason for the remarkable and enduring pleasure provided by Bruegel's imaginary landscapes and for their overwhelming authority still remains a partial mystery. If it is simply the timeless beauty of nature that illuminates them, for instance, why are they so much more profoundly absorbing than perfectly accurate views of some real and attractive corner of the world—the Delaware Water Gap, for example, seen and recorded on a golden fall day by as accomplished a painter as the 19th Century American landscape master George Inness?

Part of the answer goes back to the well-known observation that art is not truth but the illusion of truth, and to James McNeill Whistler's famous remark: "If the man who paints only the tree, or flower, or other surface he sees before him were an artist, the king of artists would be a photographer." Great paintings are not photographs but doorways into another world, a world so complete and so compelling that the eye and the mind of the viewer are drawn deeper and deeper into it. If the painting has too little content or none at all, only the eye will be pleased. Nor will the mind and the imagination be engaged in it if the content is too literal or too commonplace, stating everything but implying nothing. Such paintings, though recognizably real, will remain mere factual surfaces.

Pieter Bruegel is the great master of the walk-in painting. His final landscapes are doorways into a complex world, both cosmic and human, both beautiful and rude. It is not real, but it remains, despite the gap of centuries, recognizably ours.

Far more than with most great painters, the effect of Bruegel's work on succeeding artists was made shadowy by the flux of history and art fashion. Due to the political division in the Low Countries, what had been the single stream of Netherlandish art until Bruegel's time split soon after his death into two separate channels. Thereafter, a distinct difference existed between Dutch and Flemish painting. In Holland, newly independent, Protestant in spirit, secular and egalitarian in tone, painters turned toward small landscapes, busy winter scenes, seascapes and genre painting in which good Dutch folk might read the record of their home amusements. In such subjects the debt to Bruegel is clear enough, though in the Dutch handling Bruegel's example is more often than not reduced in scope and beauty, often to the level of mere anecdotal clutter.

In Flanders, on the other hand, Bruegel soon went out of style altogether. The territory that would one day be Belgium was transformed by Philip II during the decades after Bruegel's death into a Northern stronghold of the Catholic Counter Reformation. This was the time when Flemish artists flocked in greatest numbers to Rome, and Flanders gradually became an artistic province of the Holy City. Encouraged by the Church and the patronage of Catholic Archduke Albert who ruled in Brussels, Flemish religious art grew vast, florid and dynamic, finally ballooning into the curlicued splendors of the Baroque. What Flemish landscape painting there was tended toward the gently pastoral and eventually fell under the spell of the golden, gauzy light created by a French pastry cook-turned-landscapist named Claude Lorrain.

Bruegel was still much admired as a looming figure from the past, the last and most powerfully complete expression of the old Netherlandish tradition. But hardly more than a generation after his death he was as totally out of fashion as were the early Flemish masters. The native genius of the new Flemish age was Peter Paul Rubens. For his contemporaries he was a beakerful of the warm South frothing and overflowing from a stout Northern beer mug. Rubens sometimes borrowed from Bruegel and earlier Flemish masters, but generally, in place of silent, immobile Virgins, pale saints and Bruegel's slogging peasants, Rubens' brilliant brush conjured up pink, ample ladies who bear a satisfying family resemblance both to the soft Italianate goddesses of Renaissance art and to the stout (but rich) Antwerp matrons who so admired Rubens' pictures.

The enormous gap between Bruegel's painting and the new Baroque style can be seen in the artistic careers of the painter's two sons. Neither Pieter the Younger, born in 1564, nor Jan, born in 1568, hardly a year before his father's death, had a chance to study with their father. But they inherited scores of his drawings and compositional sketches, and were taken in hand and trained by Bruegel's gifted mother-in-law, watercolorist Mayken Verhulst.

The less talented and less successful was Pieter the Younger, and he, perhaps significantly, painted most like his father. He is now notable, in fact, only because he imitated his father so slavishly that his paintings can sometimes be used as an informal index to subjects probably painted by Pieter the Elder but now lost. Jan, on the other hand, turned to the Baroque, and in paintings like *Allegory of Sight (page 184)* satisfied his era's taste for fancy, filigreed trees and flowers and well-turned nymphs and cupids. He also collaborated with Rubens and acquired in the process six town houses in Antwerp and much contemporary acclaim.

Fashions in art can shift, if not each season as with women's hemlines, at least with each passing decade. But for more than three centuries no fashion seemed to do Pieter Bruegel's reputation much good. His landscapes and many other paintings were more or less out of circulation in Habsburg palaces in Vienna. Partly as a result, Bruegel was thought of all through the 18th and 19th Centuries as a rough-hewn painter whose work, though solid, could bear no useful comparison to the styles and standards of the great fashions in art: the High Renaissance, the Baroque, Classicism, Neo-Classicism, even Impressionism when it came along. Sir Joshua Reynolds, whose *Discourses* represent the most systematic survey of art in the 18th Century, scarcely speaks of him. John Ruskin, whose fondness both for landscape and for "primitive" painting might have led him to rediscover Bruegel for the 19th Century, does not mention him at all.

Ruskin's age, nevertheless, helped lay the groundwork for the sudden re-examination of Bruegel that occurred in our own century. For it was in the 19th Century, under the impetus of the Romantic movement, that landscape painting as a subject finally won the philosophical significance that it had lacked for so long. Man is naturally good, ran the credo of 19th Century Romanticism, but is corrupted, like everything else, by industrial society. Nature and above all natural scenery are divine. Almost overnight it became something like an act of piety to paint a hillside or a mountain or a waterfall—and landscape painting assumed an unprecedentedly respectable place in art.

Reverence for natural scenery has since declined. But landscape remains a significant subject for painters. And it was as a special kind of landscape artist that many critics in our century began to prize Pieter Bruegel. The range of their approving chorus is remarkable. It rings with the almost Wagnerian tenor of Charles de Tolnay, the best-known Bruegel scholar of modern times. For Tolnay, Bruegel's mountains are "made of the soft organic stuff of the universe," his landscapes show the earth "as a living body that moves and breathes," and constitute "the artistic representation of the 'world soul' that dwells in nature." At the other extreme is the straightforward admiration of novelist Ernest Hemingway who used to say that he learned how to write descriptions of countryside by studying landscape paintings, and who once remarked that Bruegel's landscapes stirred "an emotion that is so strong for me that I can hardly take it."

What is great art? What must great art do? No satisfactory answers have ever been found to these questions. One position, argued by Bernard Berenson, who was regarded for decades before and after World War I as *the* American oracle on art, defines great art not as something that gives pleasure but as "the reproduction of the visual images haunting great minds." Diametrically opposed, but better, perhaps, because broader, is sculptor Constantin Brancusi's gentle observation, "Don't look for obscure formulas or mysteries. It is pure joy that I am giving you. Look until you see." Many of Bruegel's paintings would qualify for greatness on either count. A handful, too, measure up to another, more demanding standard: the capacity of some great paintings to lodge so indelibly in the memory of viewers that they gradually enter the collective memory of an age.

Hunters in the Snow is such a painting. Whoever has let his eye and mind be drawn into it, first touching on those rusty, floppy-eared dogs in the foreground, then moving on down the slope past iced-over ponds and minute cottages where a chimney fire winks on a snow-covered roof as faintly crying peasants struggle to put it out, until he finally penetrates into the far distance where a winter afternoon seems to loom forever over man—that person has acquired a lifetime image. Like some phenomenon of nature, Mont Blanc, for instance, or the Grand Canyon, the best of Pieter Bruegel's paintings, once seen, become not so much visual memories as permanent possessions of the mind.

Bruegel's Seasons

Pieter Bruegel's reputation as the first great master of landscape is largely based on a series of oil panels that he painted in 1565. In them he combined two very disparate traditions with his own vision of man's place in nature to create an ageless sequence of the seasons. The early Flemish convention of decorating calendars in books with miniature scenes of outdoor work and play continued well into Bruegel's lifetime—in illustrations like those at the right by the last great master of the form, Simon Bening. Bruegel blended this tradition of exquisite smallness with a new landscape style characterized by a "cosmic" or "universal" view of the world. Artists strove to add depth and space in paintings by creating imaginary terrains as they might appear if viewed from a high hill overlooking a great distance. By joining the two approaches Bruegel created a series of fanciful landscapes, which are nevertheless a profoundly truthful portrait of man at work in the changing year. For the often stereotyped seasonal activities found in the calendar scenes he substituted a realist's sharp-eyed observations of peasant drudgery and joy. In his imaginary scenes he combined recollections of actual Alpine landscapes and the softly contoured countryside of his homeland. By expanding page-sized miniatures to panels that average 46 by 63 inches he achieved something else—sufficient scale to wed the commonplace to the ideal and fix man's daily chores against the majestic sweep of nature.

Gilt tracery frames these calendar scenes to create an illusion of size and depth, much like a view through a window. Unlike Bruegel, Bening was interested in courtly pleasures. In the garden dalliance of *April* and *May's* boating party *(top right)*, work is merely incidental. But the months below, *August* and *September,* are devoted to harvesting, fall sowing and fattening hogs on acorns.

Simon Bening: *The Months,*
c.1540

The Dark Day, 1565

The Wild Winds of March

In 16th Century Europe the calendar year began in March, not January, and this painting of half-awakened spring is the first in Bruegel's series. The lowlands have thawed, and trees along the shore are budding, but the hilltop fortress and the peaks in the background are still snow-clad. The dark clouds of an equinoctial storm race across the sky; a ship beats out of the harbor below the fortress, while others founder in the raging seas. On a foreground hill a child in a festive, pre-Lenten paper crown tugs at the hand of a woman gossiping with a man wolfing Mardi Gras waffles. Men are pruning trees and collecting willow twigs to make baskets, and a woman bundles the lopped branches. The wild weather, the melting snows and the traditional March willow pruning add up to a portrait of a spring day when the wind shakes the trees, and blood and sap begin to stir.

The Hay Harvest, 1565

The Glowing Light of June

In this radiant expression of high spring—the month of June—Bruegel centers his light-drenched landscape on the task of haymaking. Short-skirted women rake the mown grass while men stack it on a wagon. In the foreground a field hand hones a scythe in the shade of the lacy new foliage, peasants carry baskets of cherries and spring vegetables toward the village, passing a small shrine dedicated to the Virgin that is mounted on a post. Three straw-hatted women stride homeward. Beside the improbable crag across the valley, on the village green, a group of archers shoot at a target at the top of a pole. The pale glow of the fading sun spans the blue horizon. Peter Paul Rubens, who admired and collected Bruegel's work, may have been inspired by the trio of women in the foreground when he pictured a similar group in his painting *Return from the Fields*.

The Harvesters, 1565

August's Splendid Fields

Ripe stands of wheat blaze in a wide swath across Bruegel's evocation of the month of August. Blond fields in the distance at left echo the warm wheaten color under the hazy skies of high summer's hottest days, and the dark green of August's foliage breaks up the golden pattern. Men and women are harvesting the grain, binding sheaves and carrying them toward the road where a loaded wagon heads for the barn. A young man plods up the path cut through the standing wheat, bearing jugs of drink for the field workers, some already eating their noonday meal of bread, milk and fruit. One man has dozed off, his head pillowed on his jerkin. Near the cottages men are bowling on the sward, separated by a stand of fruit trees from a nude woman bather on the bank of a pond. The flat, hot, glowing scene is pure midsummer.

The Return of the Herd, 1565

October's Dying Days

Under the bare branches of the hillside trees, drovers bring their dappled cattle home from upland summer pastures, prodding their beasts down a village alley. New-thatched cottages huddle near the steepled church and step-gabled manor. The tawny meadows and russet trees of the valley frame the cool, swift river between jagged peaks. Storm clouds sweep out to smother the clear autumn sky. Peasants work in a vineyard on the lower slopes, unmoved by the gallows and wheels on the next hillock. This execution field, the fall chores and falling leaves suggest the death of the year. Perhaps it is October 31st, All Soul's Day, and Bruegel is alluding to the witches' covens of Halloween and the cruel punishment that was meted out to so many heretics, half-wits and harmless crones in his turbulent, superstitious and ruthless era.

Hunters in the Snow, 1565

The Still Depths of Winter

While nature is frozen to a standstill under glacial green skies, Bruegel's peasants enjoy the one time of the year when husbandry is not a burden. Their principal outdoor tasks are hauling firewood or tossing shovelfuls of snow on an occasional chimney fire. In the foreground, hunters, hunched against the cold, bring home a marauding fox; a puppy in their ragtag pack frisks in the snow. In front of the Inn of the Stag, a pig is being singed, foretokening a feast, and a child intently watches the fast straw fire. Bulkily bundled villagers take advantage of their rare leisure to play on the ice, practicing hockey, curling and skating. Between the matching color of the sky and ice, the pure white snow is accented only by a delicate tracery of trees. Bruegel's harsh, pale landscape, where a black bird knifes through the frigid air, is a distillation of bitter cold.

APPENDIX

Pieter Brueghel the Younger: *Landscape with Skaters and Bird Trap*, c.1626

Jan Brueghel: *Allegory of Sight*, 1617

Pieter Brueghel the Younger: *Peasant Woman Leading a Drunken Man Home,* date unknown

Jan Brueghel: *The Angler,* date unknown

Bruegel's Painter Sons

In Bruegel's time and for long after, painting was practiced as a disciplined trade that was often handed down from generation to generation—complete with patrons, paints, workshops and piles of sketches to serve as models for compositions. Not surprisingly a number of painting dynasties came into being whose members often painted very much alike. One of the most durable was founded by Bruegel—a line of artists carried his name prosperously for more than three generations, well into the mid-17th Century. Paintings by obscure members of the Brueghel family (they all spelled the name with an "h" as Bruegel originally had) still turn up in museums, looking enough like the elder Bruegel's creations to confuse an unwary visitor. Only two Bruegel descendants, however, are today regarded as noteworthy: his sons Pieter the Younger and Jan.

Pieter, born in 1564, had less talent. Although he acquired the nickname "Hell" Brueghel by painting a number of diabolic scenes inspired by Bosch and his father, he became well-to-do by copying his father's works, sometimes with almost photographic accuracy. In the copied winter landscape shown here, the son's painting never matches the crisp intensity of the father's. Where no original exists for comparison, as in the drawing of the Flemish wife dragging her sodden husband home from a tavern, the son's pictures may provide evidence that the elder Bruegel once drew the same subject.

Bruegel's younger son, Jan, had a remarkable gift for rich decoration and a taste for sartorial splendor, which won him the nickname "Velvet." Although he, too, sometimes copied from his father, he usually did so in his own way, with fresh, bright colors and an elegant, feathery line. Jan's greatest skill lay in depicting flowers, small birds and animals. He raised such things to the status of appropriate subjects for the serious artist and, in doing so, won himself a job in 1609 as court painter to the Habsburg Archduke Albert, a man much interested in the study of nature. Jan was the lifelong friend and frequent collaborator of Peter Paul Rubens. Their joint creations were idyllic scenes abounding in birds, flowers and amiable beasts, usually by Brueghel, and plump naked figures by Rubens. Jan's talents were well suited to the artistic fashions of an age much influenced by Italy and much given to Baroque spaciousness, dramatic architecture and florid beauty. A pictorial inventory of all these things is contained in his allegory *(bottom, left)* about the delights of sight—personified by the naked Venus. Around her is a mélange of things to see with and to be seen. The picture includes an imaginary art collection into which Jan incorporates one picture by his father (the horizontal seascape just behind the cupid), one by himself (the Madonna and Child wreathed in flowers) and several by Rubens. The relationship between the two men continued, in a sense, into the next generation. When Jan died in 1625, Rubens took his daughter Anna as a ward and married her off to David Teniers the Younger, who was himself the scion of a celebrated painter.

Artists of Bruegel's Era

	1400	1525	1650

NETHERLANDS

CLAUS SLUTER ?-1405/06

ROBERT CAMPIN (MASTER OF FLÉMALLE?) c.1375-1444

MELCHOIR BROEDERLAM fl.1381-1409

JAN VAN EYCK c.1390-1441

ROGER VAN DER WEYDEN 1399/1400-1464

PAUL, HERMAN AND JOHN MALOUEL DE LIMBOURG fl.1400-1430

PETRUS CHRISTUS c.1410-1472/73

DIRCK BOUTS c.1420-1475

HANS MEMLING c.1430-1494

HUGO VAN DER GOES c.1440-1482

HIERONYMUS BOSCH c.1450-1516

GERARD DAVID c.1450-1523

QUENTIN MASSYS c.1466-1530

JOACHIM PATINIR c.1475-1524

MABUSE (JAN GOSSAERT) c.1478-1532

BERNARD VAN ORLEY c.1488-1541

LUCAS VAN LEYDEN 1494-1533

JAN VAN SCOREL 1495-1562

MARTEN VAN HEEMSKERK 1498-1574

PIETER COECK VAN AELST 1502-1550

PIETER AERTSEN c.1508-1575

MATTHYS COCK c.1509-1548

HIERONYMUS COCK c.1510-1570

FRANS FLORIS 1516-1570

ANTONIS MOR (MORO) c.1517-1576/77

PIETER BRUEGEL c.1525-1569

JOACHIM BEUCKELAER c.1530-1573

MAYKEN VERHULST ?-1600

GILLIS VAN CONINXLOO 1544-1607

CAREL VAN MANDER 1548-1606

PAUL BRIL 1554-1626

HENDRICK GOLTZIUS 1558-1617

PIETER BRUEGHEL, THE YOUNGER 1564-1638

JAN BRUEGHEL 1568-1625

EGIDIUS SADELER 1570-1629

ROELAND JACOBSZ. SAVERY 1576-1639

PETER PAUL RUBENS 1577-1640

FRANS HALS 1581/85-1666

PIETER LASTMAN 1583-1633

HENDRICK AVERCAMP 1585-1634

FRANCE

JEAN FOUQUET 1420-1477/81   JAN VAN GOYEN 1596-1656

NICOLAS FROMENT fl.1450-1490

MAÎTRE DE MOULINS fl.1480-1500

JEAN CLOUET c.1486-1541

	1400	1525	1650

GERMANY

HANS MULTSCHER c.1400-1467

STEPHAN LOCHNER fl.1410-1451

MEISTER FRANCKE fl.1424-1435

LUCAS MOSER fl.1431-1440

MICHAEL PACHER c.1435-1498

MARTIN SCHONGAUER c.1450-1491

HANS HOLBEIN, THE ELDER 1460/65-1524

GRÜNEWALD (MATHIS NITHART GOTHART) c.1470-1528

ALBRECHT DÜRER 1471-1528

LUCAS CRANACH, THE ELDER 1472-1553

HANS BURGKMAIR 1473-1531

ALBRECHT ALTDORFER c.1480-1538

HANS BALDUNG GRIEN 1480-1545

HANS HOLBEIN, THE YOUNGER c.1498-1543

ITALY

FRA ANGELICO 1400-1455

JACOPO BELLINI c.1400-c.1470

PIERO DELLA FRANCESCA 1410/20-1492

ANTONELLO DA MESSINA 1414/30-1479/93

GENTILE BELLINI 1429-1507

GIOVANNI BELLINI c.1430-1516

ANDREA MANTEGNA 1431-1506

ANTONIO POLLAIUOLO 1433-1498

SANDRO BOTTICELLI 1444-1510

PERUGINO (PIETRO VANNUCCI) 1446/47-1523

DOMENICO GHIRLANDAIO 1449-1494

VITTORE CARPACCIO c.1450-c.1525

LEONARDO DA VINCI 1452-1519

MICHELANGELO BUONARROTI 1475-1564

GIORGIONE DA CASTELFRANCO 1477/78-1510

RAPHAËL URBINAS 1483-1520

ANDREA DEL SARTO 1486/88-1530

TITIAN (TIZIANO VERCELLIO) c.1488-1576

JACOPO DA PONTORMO 1493/94-1557/58

GIULIO CLOVIO 1498-1578

PARMIGIANINO (GIROLAMO MAZZOLA) 1503-1540

GIORGIO VASARI 1511-1574

TINTORETTO (JACOPO ROBUSTI) 1518-1594

VERONESE (PAOLO CALIARI) 1528-1588

GIANLORENZO BERNINI 1598-1680

SPAIN

BERNARDO MARTORELL fl.1433-1453

BARTOLOMÉ BERMEJO fl.1474-1495

LUIS MORALES c.1509-1586

ALONSO SANCHEZ COELLO 1515-1590

EL GRECO (DOMENIKOS THEOTOCOPOULOS) 1540/50-1614

	1400	1525	1650

Bruegel's predecessors, contemporaries and successors are grouped here in chronological order according to country. The bands correspond to the lifespans of the artists or, where this information is unknown, to the approximate periods when they flourished (indicated by the abbreviation "fl.").

Bibliography ★Paperback

BRUEGEL—HIS LIFE AND WORKS

Arpino, Giovanni and Piero Bianconi (editors), *L'Opera Completa di Bruegel*. Rizzoli Editore, Milan, 1967.

Denis, Valentin (editor), *All the Paintings of Pieter Bruegel*. Translated by Paul Colacicchi. Oldbourne Press, 1961.

Glück, Gustav, *Peter Brueghel the Elder*. Thames & Hudson, 1958.

Grossman, F., *Bruegel: Complete Edition of His Paintings*. Phaidon Press, 1966.

Klein, H. Arthur, *Graphic Worlds of Peter Bruegel the Elder*.★ Dover Publications, Inc., . New York, 1963.

Lavalleye, Jacques, *Pieter Bruegel the Elder and Lucas van Leyden: The Complete Engravings, Etchings, and Woodcuts*. Thames & Hudson, 1967.

Le Siècle de Bruegel (exhibition catalogue). Musées Royaux des Beaux-Arts de Belgique, Brussels, 1963.

Münz, L., *Bruegel, Drawings—A Complete Edition*. Phaidon Press, 1961.

Prints and Drawings of Pieter Bruegel the Elder (exhibition catalogue). Los Angeles County Museum, Los Angeles, California, 1961.

Stordbeck, C. G., *Bruegel Studien*, Stockholm, 1956.

Tolnay, Charles de, *Pierre Bruegel L'Ancien*. Nouvelle Société d'Editions, Brussels, 1935.

ON OTHER PAINTERS

Baldass, Ludwig von, *Hieronymus Bosch*. Thames & Hudson, 1960.

Buzzati, Dino (editor), *L'Opera Completa di Bosch*. Rizzoli Editore, Milan, 1966.

Delevoy, Robert L., *Bosch*. Translated by Stuart Gilbert. Albert Skira, Geneva, 1960.

Fränger, Wilhelm, *The Millennium of Hieronymus Bosch*. Faber & Faber, 1952.

Friedländer, Max J., *From Van Eyck to Bruegel*. Phaidon Press, 1969.

Lassaigne, Jacques and Robert L. Delevoy, *Flemish Painting from Bosch to Rubens*. Albert Skira, Geneva, 1958.

Lassaigne, Jacques, *Flemish Painting: The Century of Van Eyck*. Albert Skira, Geneva, 1957.

Philip, Lotte Brand, *Hieronymus Bosch*. Thames & Hudson, 1955.

Read, Sir Herbert, *Hieronymus Bosch*. 'The Masters' Series No. 66, Purnell & Sons Limited, 1967.

Tolnay, Charles de, *Hieronymus Bosch*. Reynal & Company, Inc., Clifton, N.Y., 1966.

Venturi, Lionello, *The Sixteenth Century from Leonardo to El Greco*. Albert Skira, Geneva, 1956.

CULTURAL AND HISTORICAL BACKGROUND

Blok, Petrus Johannes, *A History of the People of the Netherlands*, vol. 3. Translated by Ruth Putnam. G. P. Putnam's Sons, 1912.

Dolan, John P. (ed.), *The Essential Erasmus*.★ Selected and translated with introduction and commentary by John P. Dolan. Mentor Books: The New English Library, 1966.

Evans, Joan, *The Flowering of the Middle Ages*. Thames & Hudson, 1966.

Geyl, Pieter, *Debates with Historians*.★ Fontana Books: S. Collins, 1962.

The Revolt of the Netherlands: 1555-1609.★ Ernest Benn Limited, 1966.

Harbison, E. Harris, *The Age of Reformation*.★ Cornell University Press, Ithaca, New York, 1955.

Huizinga, J., *Erasmus of Rotterdam*. Phaidon Press, 1952.

The Waning of the Middle Ages.★ Penguin, 1965.

Lucas, Henry, *The Renaissance and the Reformation*, second edition. Harper & Row, 1964.

Meeüs, Adrien de, *History of the Belgians*. Translated by G. Gerdon. Thames & Hudson, 1962.

Murray, Margaret Alice. *The Witch Cult in Western Europe*.★ Oxford University Press, 1963.

Nigg, Walter, *The Heretics*. Edited and translated by Richard and Clara Winston. Alfred A. Knopf, New York, 1962.

Petrie, Sir Charles, *Philip II of Spain*. Eyre & Spottiswoode, 1963.

Phillips, Margaret Mann, *Erasmus and the Northern Renaissance*.★ Cambridge University Press, 1968.

Postan, M. and H. J. Habakkuk (editors), *The Cambridge Economic History of Europe*, vols. 2 and 4. Cambridge University Press, 1952.

Smith, Preserved, *Reformation in Europe*.★ Macmillan, 1962.

Spengler, Oswald, *The Decline of the West*. Allen & Unwin, 1962.

Vaughan, Richard, *Philip the Bold: The Formation of the Burgundian State*. Harvard University Press, Cambridge, Mass., 1962.

Wedgwood, C. V., *William the Silent*. Bedford Historical Series, Jonathan Cape, 1967.

ART-HISTORICAL BACKGROUND

Benesch, Otto, *The Art of the Renaissance in Northern Europe*, revised edition. Phaidon Press, 1965.

Clark, Kenneth, *Landscape into Art*.★ John Murray, 1949.

Ferguson, George, *Signs and Symbols in Christian Art*.★ Oxford University Press, 1961.

Flanders in the Fifteenth Century: Art and Civilization, Catalogue of the Exhibition: Masterpieces of Flemish Art—Van Eyck to Bosch. The Detroit Institute of Arts, Detroit, Michigan, 1960.

Friedländer, Max J., *Landscape, Portrait, Still-life*.★ Schocken Books, New York, 1963.

Mâle, Emile, *Religious Art from the Twelfth to the Eighteenth Century*.★ Routledge and Kegan Paul, 1949.

Panofsky, Erwin, *Early Netherlandish Painting: Its Origins and Character* (2 vols.). Oxford University Press, 1958.

Roy, Claude, *Arts Fantastiques*. Delpire, Paris, 1960.

Stechow, Wolfgang, *Dutch Landscape Painting of the Seventeenth Century*. Phaidon Press, 1966.

Northern Renaissance Art, 1400-1600.★ Prentice-Hall, Inc., Englewood Cliffs, New Jersey, 1966.

Tovell, Ruth Massey, *Flemish Artists of the Valois Courts*. University of Toronto Press, Toronto, 1950.

Van Mander, Carel, *Le Livre de Peinture*.★ Paris, 1965.

Picture Credits

The sources for the illustrations in this book appear below. Credits for pictures from left to right are separated by semicolons, from top to bottom by dashes.

COVER: Erich Lessing from Magnum

END PAPERS: Staatliche Museen, Berlin, Kupferstichkabinett

INTRODUCTION: 9—Erich Lessing from Magnum. 10,11—Eric Schaal except Erich Lessing from Magnum middle and right.
CHAPTER 1: 12—Erich Lessing from Magnum. 16—© A.C.L. Brussels. 17—Alinari. 23—The Guennol Collection courtesy The Pierpont Morgan Library (2). 24, 25—Maps by Rafael Palacios (2). 29—Eric Schaal. 30—National Gallery, London. 31—Foto Blauel. 32, 33—National Gallery, London (2). 34, 35—Eric Schaal. 36, 37—Scala (2). 38—National Gallery, London. 39—National Gallery of Art, Washington, D.C.
CHAPTER 2: 40—National Gallery, London. 42—Giraudon. 47—From *Les Genre Satirique dans la Peinture Flamande*, Louis Maeterlinck, 1903, Ghent. 50, 51—Giraudon (2). 53—© Max Seidel, Mittenwald. 55, 56—Bildarchiv der Nationalbibliothek, Vienna (2). 57—Eddy van der Veen. 58, 59—Scala. 60, 61—Fernand Bourges—Scala. 62—Scala. 63—Lee Boltin. 64, 65—Editions d'Art Albert Skira. 66, 67—Mayer van den Bergh Museum, Antwerp.
CHAPTER 3: 68—Staatliche Museen, Berlin, Gemaeldegalerie. 71—Bildarchiv der Nationalbibliothek, Vienna. 74—By permission of the Trustees of the Chatsworth Settlement. 76—New York Public Library. 78—© Rijksmuseum, Amsterdam —A.C.L. Brussels (2). 81-87—© Koninklijke Bibliotheek, Brussels.
CHAPTER 4: 88—National Gallery, London. 91—Alinari. 95—Bildarchiv der Nationalbibliothek, Vienna. 97—By courtesy of the Trustees of the British Museum—Biblioteca Nazionale Marciana, Venice. 98—From *Novae Theoricae Planetarum*, Georg Peurbach, 1534, Venice. 99—From *De Revolutionibus Orbium Celestium*, Nicolas Copernicus, 1566 Edition. 101—Erich Lessing from Magnum. 102—Scala. 103-111—Erich Lessing from Magnum (8).
CHAPTER 5: 112-Erich Lessing from Magnum. 114, 115—Frank Lerner from Lerner-Raymond (10). 116—Bildarchiv der Nationalbibliothek, Vienna. 119—From *Andreae Vesalii Bruxellensis Icones Anatomicae*, 1934, The Library of the University of Munich and The New York Academy of Medicine. (2). 120—Scala. 123—The Metropolitan Museum of Art. 125—Staatliche Museen, Berlin, Kupferstichkabinett. 126—Bildarchiv der Nationalbibliothek, Vienna. 127—Dresden Kupferstichkabinett courtesy Deutsche Fotothek; Staedelsches Kunstinstitut, Frankfurt am Main—Boymans-van Beuningen Museum, Rotterdam. 128—Boymans-van Beuningen Museum, Rotterdam. 129—Foto Blauel. 130-131—Frank Lerner from Lerner-Raymond. 132, 133—Agraci. 134-139—Erich Lessing from Magnum (3).
CHAPTER 6: 140—Marzari. 142—Walters Art Gallery. 144—© Rijksmuseum, Amsterdam. 145—No Credit. 147—© A.C.L. Brussels (2). 151-159—Staatliche Museen, Berlin, Gemaeldegalerie. (6).
CHAPTER 7: 160—Giraudon. 165—The Metropolitan Museum of Art. 168—Achenbach Foundation for Graphic Arts. 173—Alan Clifton (4). 174, 175—Erich Lessing from Magnum (2). 176, 177—Harry Redl (2). 178, 179—Robert S. Crandall (2). 180-183—Erich Lessing from Magnum (4).
APPENDIX: 184—Marzari—Lee Boltin. 185—Staedelsches Kunstinstitut, Frankfurt am Main—© Koninklijke Bibliotheek, Brussels.

Acknowledgments

For their help in the production of this book the author and editors wish to thank the following people: Director Erwin M. Auer and George J. Kugler, Kunsthistorisches Museum, Vienna; Biblioteca Nazionale Marciana, Venice; Nicolas Calas; Harriet Cooper, Deanna Cross, James Humphrey III and James Parker, The Metropolitan Museum of Art; Marie-Lucie Cornillot, Conservateur, Musées de Besançon; F. Delporte; Martha Durham; Fritz Grossmann, Director, Manchester Museum of Art, Manchester, England; Madame Guynet-Péchadre, Conservateur, Service Photographique, Musée du Louvre, Paris; Marianne Haraszti, Museum of Fine Arts, Budapest; Joseph Jobé, Edita, Lausanne; Ivan Kats, Yale University; Director Walter Koschatzky, Konrad Oberhuber and Renate Antonio, Graphische Sammlung Albertina, Vienna; Marie-Thérèse Liebermann; Henner Menz, Staatliche Kunstsammlungen, Dresden; Museum Boymans-van Beuningen, Rotterdam; Lotte Brand Philip, Associate Professor of Art, Queens College of the City University of New York; Rijksmuseum, Amsterdam; Staatliche Museen Kupferstichkabinett, Berlin; Richard Tooke, Museum of Modern Art; A.A. van der Heyden, Elsevier, Amsterdam; Director G. van Roey and R. van de Weghe, Municipal Archives, Antwerp.

Index

Numerals in italics indicate a picture. Unless otherwise identified, all listed art works are by Bruegel. Dimensions are given in inches; height precedes width.

Index (continued)

Printed in Spain by Printer industria gráfica sa   Provenza 388, 5.ª   Barcelona-25   Depósito legal 20837-1978